The E-Commerce Bubble

What Every Entrepreneur Needs to Know
About Starting an Online Business

By: Brandon Cutler

Introduction

This book contains proven steps and strategies on how to earn both passive and active income and finally become financially independent from online business. With the help of this book, you will learn about making money through a variety of income streams.

This book contains details about the popular online money making opportunities available today. If you follow the steps written in this book, you will eventually achieve what pretty much everyone wants: income on your own terms. Work from anywhere you want, whenever you want.

Now is the perfect time to get started making money online, as there are many opportunities out there. If you are not taking advantage of them, then you may be missing out on something that could make all the difference. I know that it may seem daunting to find the right path at first, as the e-commerce world is so overwhelmingly large and extremely competitive, and it's difficult to know where to start sometimes.

Before you leap into any project, you must realize that not every online opportunity is legitimate. There are many scams out there, and that is something I have to warn you about at the start. To separate the genuine opportunities from the scams, here are some little pearls of wisdom you may find useful.

Always start looking for those choices and

opportunities that are free. If you have to invest a large amount of cash, to begin with, it's better to look elsewhere. They may not necessarily be cons, as there are many programs that require an initial investment, but there is a very good chance that you will never see your money returned.

Instead look for those choices that offer a slow and steady payment. Don't fall victim to all of those get rich quick schemes that offer you millions of dollars in profits. These are almost certain to be scams. The real opportunities will normally only allow you to make money in a slow but steady way that increases as your business grows, and not in the rollercoaster ride style of the get rich quick scheme.

Now that you have been warned about the scams, it is the time that we consider your choices. You already know that you have many different paths to choose from, but how do you choose the right one? First, you should consider what it is that you enjoy doing, and any things that you are good at, and then think about how much time you have to invest.

If you only want an income to supplement your current wage, then you will need to choose an option that will only require a relatively tiny amount of daily work, such as placing adverts for other businesses on your blog or website. If, on the other hand, you want an income that can replace your current wage, you could consider writing content for companies on blogs or even providing leads and referrals for companies to find new customers.

Once you make the decision as to the type of work that you are willing to do, you will then only have to find that work online. You are already aware of what you should avoid when considering the online opportunities available, so now you will be better able to choose the correct option for you. You may find that what started as only supplemental income could become a full-time endeavor and the money you earn from it far exceeds anything you previously thought you could earn.

Section 1: Blogging and Content Marketing

What is Blogging?

Before understanding – Why and How to Blog, you should know about why blogging is getting so popular--Why people all over the world love to read blogs and why so many people are starting them?

In short, we can say that Blogging is the best way to publicize your views, thoughts and experiences to the world in a short span of time.

In this modern era, being tech savvy and internet proficient has become essential to keeping up with the speed at which we are advancing. Everything has become so much faster, more transparent and easier to use.

Let's just talk about the most popular online writing method called blogging. Blogging can either be professional or general/individual if categorized by the idea behind its creation.

Blogging is a unique way to socialize with readers and to spread information across a network of friends, and followers. Blogging presents an easy, decent and free way to exchange ideas and views about everything in this world.

Why and How to Blog?

Blogging is an online platform which connects the writer and the reader of the blogs, to write and read about something particular. It also helps form a network of contacts for commercial and personal use in future.

Blogging has become the latest obsession of internet savvy people all around the globe. You can easily start a blog about anything under the sun, although just because you can write about something, doesn't mean that will be a profitable blogging topic (but we'll get to that later). So, if you have the flair for writing, you should consider blogging for sure.

Go to any search engine, type in some keywords and you'll find the first page is filled with blog posts and articles. These are the types of websites that always seem to rank the highest with search engines like Google. You will quickly see that there are many many tens of thousands of blogs out there.

And this number is continuously increasing day after day.

Today with a list of free blogging platforms, you can sign up and join the team of great bloggers for free.

You get your own personal URL address that you can

use to gain worldwide exposure just sitting and writing at your home.

Both online and brick and mortar type businesses blogging strategies to market their products and services although many of them do not do it successfully because they don't take the time to learn how to be successful with blogging.

Finding your niche:

One of the biggest problems most aspiring bloggers grapple with is deciding what to write about. Actually, this is one of the most important decisions you will make when starting your blog. It is a major determinant of your blog's success or failure, and therefore, you need to ensure that you get it right.

It is important that you blog about a specific topic. If you decide to blog about everything under the sun, you will never run out of content. However, it will be very hard for you to build recurrent targeted traffic, and even harder for you to make money off your blog. This is why you will notice that the most popular and successful blogs identify themselves around one of these categories:

- A specific niche
- A specific demographic
- A particular challenge people have

So, how do you choose a niche that you should blog about? If you look this up on the internet, you will notice that nearly every resource mentions three things: passion, traffic, and profitability.

Well, this makes sense. If you don't have passion, chances are that you will abandon your blog before you even start making money. You might write for a couple months and run out of steam. In these cases, you need passion to keep you going. However, I believe that people can be passionate about anything that is going to make them some money. Plus, you could be passionate about a number of things. Should you blog about all your passions? Probably not.

Traffic is important, because you don't want to create a blog that will only be read by your friends and family. Choosing a niche with high traffic ensures you have a lot of people looking for information about related topics. However, you don't need tons of traffic to make money off your blog. Some blogs make decent enough money with a relatively small audience while others have big audiences and still earn disappointing incomes.

Lastly, profitability. To me, this is the most important factor, because regardless of whatever you achieve with your blog, it is still a business, and needs to make money. You therefore need to blog about a topic around which people are willing to spend money.

From the above, it is clear that while having lots of passion and a ton of traffic around your idea is an added advantage, lack of the same doesn't mean that you can't make money off your blog. The most important thing for your chosen niche is the potential for profitability. People should be willing to spend money in your niche.

So, how do you ensure that your chosen topic will help you make money?

Before I get into how you can go about choosing a profitable niche, I will share something very important that you need to keep in mind. When starting a blog, you should understand that you are not writing for yourself. You are writing for your readers. It is therefore important that you have good knowledge of your target audience, what they like (or despise), and what attracts them to a blog.

Listed here are some of the things that readers want from a blog:

They want to solve a problem. Most people searching for information on the internet have a problem that is bothering them. If you choose to blog about a problem that is common to a number of people and provide a solution that works, you are assured two things: traffic and profitability. There will be a number of people searching for a solution to this problem, and some of them will be willing to pay you if you can take their problem away.

They want to learn something new. Nowadays, when people want to learn something new, they rarely go to a formal class. Instead, they head to the internet to see if they can learn by themselves. If you can effectively teach people something that they are trying to learn, then you already have something to blog about. Is there something you are good at that your peers or colleagues always ask you to help them with? Think of how many other people are faced with the same challenge. You can show them how to go about it on your blog.

They want to reach their goals. Many people have goals they want to reach, but at times they don't know how. Or maybe they know how but lack the motivation to push through. Do you have a goal that you have set and achieved? Are there others struggling with the same thing? You can share with them how you achieved your goal and inspire them to push through with to reach theirs.

After choosing an idea that addresses one of these needs, you can then test it for traffic and profitability. How do you do this?

Testing Your Idea for Traffic and Profitability

Find the Search Volume for Your Niche Idea

While it is possible to make money even with a small audience, it is always good to ensure that there is sufficient traffic to keep you going. Therefore, finding the number of people who are searching for things related to your niche idea is a great first step. Since Google is the largest search engine, you should focus on the number of searches done on Google. You can do this using the Google Keyword Planner Tool, which is free tool provided by Google to help people get search data. Simply sign up for an account, click on the

"Get search volume data and trends" button and enter your niche idea. You might opt to get data for a specific location or general data for all locations. Once you press the "get search volume" button, you will get data about the number of people searching for your niche idea every month.

This step will give you a general idea of the amount of demand for your niche idea. Keep in mind that this is not keyword research or competitor analysis. You simply want to know if people care about your niche idea. The broader your niche, the more the search volume you want to see, otherwise you might be in a small niche that doesn't have much demand.

Check Google Trends

Once you know that there is some demand for your niche, the next step is to find out if there is evergreen demand for the niche. To do this, simply go to http://www.google.com/trends and enter your niche idea. This will help you determine if the demand for your niche is rising, falling or stable. Avoid niche ideas with decreasing demand. This step will also help you identify niches that have seasonal demand. You should take the time to understand the reason behind a niche's spike or fall in demand. For instance, some products might have had a spike due to media attention. Such things might mislead you if you don't take time to understand the reason behind these trends. For example, finding out that a niche is not as popular as it once was does not automatically mean that it is no longer profitable. It might simply have gained popularity at a particular time because it went viral, or because it is a seasonal niche.

Find Out If There Are Products On Sale Within The Niche

If a niche is profitable, you will find lots of physical and digital products on sale within the niche. On the other hand, lack of products related to a niche is a sign that there is not money to be made within the niche. You can check for the availability of products related to a niche on sites like Amazon, ShareASale, Ebay, JVZoo, Clickbank, and CJ.com. In this step, you are not looking for a specific volume. Instead, you just want some proof that people spend money in this niche and in what volumes. For instance, you can use Amazon to search for physical products while Clickbank is good for digital products. You can also look for products on Google. Simply Google your niche and check if the ranking websites are selling any products. If you find that a niche has several products on sale across multiple networks, it is a sign that you are onto a profitable idea. However, you need to go a step further and find out if you can personally make money within the niche. Landing on a profitable niche does not mean that you will automatically make money.

Validate Online Activity Through Popular Websites And Blogs

A niche that has several authority sites and blogs shows that there are a lot of customers in the niche and places to find them. In this step, you want to find sites where potential customers hang out so you can target traffic from these sites. Simply go to the Google search bar and type in your niche idea. Alternatively, you can search for terms like "best {niche idea} blogs" to find the top blogs within the niche. Once you identify the top blogs, find out whether their articles attract a lot of comments and social shares and whether they have a following on social media. What do they sell and how do they make money? This will give you an idea of how interactive the niche is and how easy it will be to connect with customers within the niche.

Find Forums And Message Boards Around The Niche

A niche that has sizable forums and niches around it with active members shows that there is a huge crowd of people who are passionate about the niche and willing to hold discussions around it. Typically, people who are passionate about a topic are always willing to spend money on it. You can find forums and message boards through Google or through sites like FindAForum.net. If you find sizable and active forums, this is a sure sign that there is money to be made in the niche.

Are There Social Media Hubs?

The next step is to find out if there is any activity surrounding your chosen niche on social media sites like Facebook. If there are pages and groups on social media dedicated to a niche, that is a clear sign that the niche has an interactive community who likes to connect. These are all potential customers. Once you start your blog, you can share your content to these groups to drive traffic to your blog. Do not restrict yourself to Facebook. Check for your niche on all social media sites, including Instagram, Twitter, Pinterest, Tumblr, Google Plus, Reddit, and so on.

Are People Advertising On Google?

Finally, are there any ads when you search for you niche on Google? A lot of ads is a good sign. Generally, people only pay for advertisements if they know they will make their money back. Although, nowadays, many people invest in google ads without knowing what they're doing and without doing proper research first, so this is only a general guideline and not a hard and fast rule. But generally, if people are paying for Google Ads to advertise their products within that niche, this shows that there is money to be made in the niche.

By running through these steps, you will be able to validate whether your chosen niche is profitable. One thing you should keep in mind is that coming up with a new niche is next to impossible. Therefore, if you find a niche without any products or without other people, it doesn't mean that you have stumbled on an untapped niche. On the contrary, it might mean that there is no money to be made in that niche or that—quite simply, no one is interested in this. You may argue that there are always at least "some" people interested in any given thing, but then you have to consider the cost and difficulty in tracking down and connecting with these people. If there's no activity around this "niche" already, it may be a lot of work to start generating that activity on your own. A profitable niche will have a significant number of searches, lots of products that sell well, lots of other blogs and websites on the niche, lots of forums and social media activity, as well as people who are paying to advertise products and services related to the niche. Don't mistake my advice in this section for me telling you not to try anything new. I'm merely suggesting that if you're just starting out with an online business or blog, it's better to start in a market niche where you know there is demand and money to be made. However, you have to also consider that these markets become more and more saturated and more and more flooded with competition. This means you simply offering what everyone else is already offering won't cut it. You need to show the audience that you have something different or better—but more on that later.

Getting Started:

Choosing the Right Name For Your Blog

Coming up with the right name for your blog is very important. It determines the future of your blog and how your visitors will relate to you blog. Unfortunately, for many people, coming up with a good blog name is not an easy task. Many are the times you will come up with the perfect name only to conduct a domain search and find out that someone else thought of it long before you. Other bloggers will come up with a name that does not relate to their niche. A good blog name should help potential visitors understand what your blog is about, even without visiting the blog. We are going to look at the process you should follow to come up with a great name for your blog.

It's always advisable to use your blog name as your domain name; therefore, in this guide, there will be an overlap between the blog name and the domain name.

Before we dive in, we need to define something. What makes a good name?

> ➢ It should be catchy and memorable.
> ➢ It should be short and concise.
> ➢ People should be able to read and pronounce it easily.

➤ People should be able to spell it easily.

➤ It should help people understand the theme of your blog.

➤ Opt for a .com domain extension.

Why I Don't Like Blog Name Generators

If you want to avoid the process of coming up with a name for your blog, you can always use a name generator. You simply put in the keywords that describe your blog and it will generate suggestions for you. However, I do not recommend using a blog name generator. I would only advise you to use one if you are looking for a lackluster name for your blog. Blog name generators simply create mash-ups of the words you enter; therefore, they are unlikely to produce any worthwhile names. Unless you are extremely lazy, avoid using blog name generators.

How to Come Up with A Good Blog Name

Now that we know what we are aiming for, let's get down to the process of coming up with the perfect name for your blog. We are going to break down this process into two steps:

➤ Explore the theme of your blog.

➤ Vet your chosen name.

Explore the Theme of Your Blog

Remember, I said that a good blog name should help potential visitors understand the theme of your blog. This first part involves exploring your blog's theme to come up with name ideas.

Write Down a List of Topics Related to Your Blog

Create a list of the topics you will be blogging about, as well as any other words that are associated with those topics. For instance, if you want to blog about cars, you might come up with words like automobile, tires, engine, motor, driving, speed, petrol, diesel, gear, alloy wheels, drivetrain, sedan, truck, traffic, etc.

The idea is to come up with as many words as you can. Even if you know you are not going to use some of these words, coming up with this list will help spark ideas. Once you are done with the list, cross out the words that you don't want as part of your blog name.

Think of Your Blog's Tone

Next, take a moment to explore your blog's tone. Your blog's tone is basically how you want your blog to feel and the mood you want it to exude. Tone is defined not by what you say, but by how you say it. It includes your choice of words, how they are arranged, and their rhythm. Blog tones can be casual, serious, funny, sarcastic, you name it.

Once you identify your tone, create another list of words that describe your tone. This will help you come up with a name that matches the feel of your blog.

Think of Your Target Audience

Next, you need to define your target audience. Who do you want to read your blog? Young dads? Biking enthusiasts? Writers? Think of what your target audience will be seeking on your blog. List the characteristics of your target audience, as well as some of the things they hope to get out of your blog. This step will help you come up with a name that resonates with your readers.

Research the Competition

Look at blogs in the same niche as you and how they are named. The aim of this step is not to steal your competitors' names, but rather to help point your creativity in the right direction. This step will give you a better idea of the kind of names that work and those that do not.

Come Up with A List of Blog Name Ideas

By now, I'm hoping that you have three lists of words. Go through the lists again and cross out any words that you do not want as part of your blog name. Try coming up with blog name ideas from the remaining words. Now is the time to get creative. Try pairing together two words from different lists. Add a creative prefix or suffix to some words. Play around with the words to create your own new words or add a touch of humor. You can also try using alliteration. For instance, if your blog is aimed at successful young ladies, you could name it "Sweet, Sassy, and Successful." Think outside the box and come up with as many ideas as you can.

Narrow Down Your List

Go through the list of blog name ideas you came up with in the previous step and choose those you think might work. This should be based on your blog's tone, target audience, readability, ease of spelling and pronunciation, as well as memorability.

By the end of this step, you should have three to five appropriate names. Now it's time for step two of our process.

Vet Your Chosen Names

In this step, you will be evaluating your chosen names to make sure they meet all the requirements before making your choice.

The Domain Test

As I mentioned earlier, one of the worst things is coming up with the perfect blog name only to find out that someone else is already using it. Before you proceed, now is the time to check your chosen domains for availability. If two are already taken and the third one is free, your choice has been made for you. If none are available, you will have to go back to the drawing board.

Even if you find that the .com extension of your chosen domain is available, it is important to check the .net and .org extensions of your name to make sure that there aren't other organizations using the same name.

You should also consider how your chosen names look when used as domain names, so you do not end up with an unintentionally inappropriate domain name, such as whorepresents.com (Who Represents) or powergenitalia.com (Powergen Italia). Those are real sites, by the way.

Does the Name Have Staying Power?

Will your chosen name still be relevant a few years down the road? Will it be relevant if you decide to broaden the focus of your blog? Is it bound by a geographical location? For instance, if your blog is aimed at bike riders in Cincinnati and has the name Cincinnati as part of its name, what happens when you want to target riders outside Cincinnati? You should also avoid using trendy words, since that will make your blog seem outdated once the trend shifts to something else.

Does the Name Need a Disclaimer?

When coming up with a name for your blog, think about the long-term growth of your blog. For instance, you could be running a blog for guys who are learning how to play the guitar, but down the road you know that you might start blogging about other instruments as well. In this case, you should avoid using the word guitar in your blog name so you don't have to word the disclaimer: "Well, it's not just for learning the guitar." Ensure that that your blog name doesn't force you to explain that your blog is not what is seems.

Make Your Final Choice

Finally, if a name has made it this far, then you have yourself the right name for your blog. If two or more names made it, then go with the one that feels like the best one for you.

Whether you are searching for a name for your new blog or whether you want to rebrand an existing blog, the process shared will help you come up with a good name that you won't regret down the road.

Setting Up Your Blog:

You are going to learn how to choose the right blogging platform and how to set up your blog. Now that you have settled on the niche you are going to blog about and have chosen a name for your blog, it is time for you to get down to the actual business of setting up your blog.

Choosing The Best Blogging Platform

The first thing you need to do is to choose the blogging platform that you are going to use for your blog. A blogging platform is a service of software that allows you to publish your content online. It is also a content management system (CMS) that allows you to manage your online content. The kind of blogging platform you opt for depends on how tech savvy you are, as well as the kind of blog you want to build.

Choosing the most appropriate blogging platform is very important. This is because switching from one platform to another can be a headache. If you start on one platform and then later decide that you want to have some features on your blog that are not supported by your current platform, then it will take you a lot of effort and money to move your already-growing blog to another platform. It might also have some implications on your blog's traffic. Therefore, the best thing to do is to ensure that you choose the best platform for you from the very start.

To ensure that you pick the right blogging platform from the beginning of your blogging career, here are some things that you should consider:

Your Goals

The first thing you need to consider before settling on a blogging platform is what you aspire to achieve through your blog. Determining you goals when you are just starting can be a difficult thing to do. However, it will save you a lot of trouble down the road. To help you determine what you want to achieve from your blog, you can ask yourself questions such as:

> ➢ Do I intend to blog long-term?
> ➢ How do I intend to monetize my blog?
> ➢ Is there a chance that I might serve ads

on my blog?

Such questions will help you figure out your goals for the blog. You can think of other such questions that take a long-term view at your blogging career. Doing this is very important, because different blogging platforms are better suited for different blogging applications.

Budget

Your choice of blogging platform will also be affected by the amount of money you are willing to spend. When it comes to blogging, there are three main things you might be required to pay for. These are your domain name, hosting for your blog, and the blogging platform you choose to use. However, different blogging platforms have different approaches to this. For instance, some platforms like WordPress.com and Blogger.com are free. This means that you get a domain name, hosting, and access to the platform without having to pay a dime. With others like

WordPress.org (this is a different platform from WordPress.com), you get free access to the platform, but then you have to find and pay for your own domain name and hosting. Other platforms like MovableType have a free version as well as a paid version depending on your application of the platform. MovableType also requires you to find your own domain name and hosting.

Apart from paying for the platform, domain name, and hosting, other costs you might incur when setting up your blog include:

Design: All blogging platforms provide free templates that you can apply on your blog. However, if you want a more unique look for your blog, you will need to come up with your own design. If you do not have some web design skills, you will need to hire someone to design the blog for you.

In most cases I strongly recommend that you hire a designer. Most people do not have sufficient graphic design expertise to design their own logos/graphics/web layouts. Considering that this is one of the most important investments you'll make in your business, you don't want to cut corners here. When people visit your site, they will immediately judge if they think it's worth staying on your website by the quality of your site. If your page looks very amateur and "homemade," people will most likely exit out and move on to the next thing because they won't trust that you're really a reputable source of information.

You can find very affordable designers on websites like Fiverr and Upwork.

Blog tools: If you want to build a profitable blog, you will need access to some tools to make your work easier and to help you track your blog's progress. While some of these tools are free, you will need to pay for others. At the beginning, you might not really need these tools, but they will definitely come in handy as your blog grows. Do some research on what type of tools will help you the most in running your blog—the recommended tools vary from person to person and depend on the actual topic and format of your blog.

Your Technological Know-How

This is another important factor that has a major bearing on your choice of blogging platform. Some blogging platforms are quite technical and complicated, and therefore might be a huge challenge for someone who is trying to build a blog for the first time. Other platforms are a lot simpler and can be used even by beginners, provided you are willing to learn a few basic things.

Of course, even if you are not very technically aligned, you can find someone who is more knowledgeable to lend you a hand. The great thing with blogging is that there is a wide base of communal knowledge around the subject, so you can just join a forum and learn everything you need to know about your chosen platform.

Remember, that there are pros and cons to both types of platforms. The super technical platforms are much more customizable—that means that you can change and adapt anything on your blog so that it perfectly fits your vision. On the simple platforms, while they're very easy to use and require very little technical skill, you'll have to be satisfied with templates and standards already in place. Many of these templates have formatting that you really can't change. For some people this is no problem, but for others it really defeats the purpose, so you'll have to decide what's best for your needs.

Choosing Between a Hosted and A Standalone Blogging Platform

I mentioned earlier that some blogging platforms will provide you with free hosting (hosted platforms), while others require you to find and pay for your own hosting (standalone platforms). So, what is the difference between the two, and which of them is better?

Hosted Blogging Platforms

Most bloggers start with this kind of platforms, the reason being that such platforms are usually free (or very cheap) and are very easy to use. The most popular hosted blogging platform is Google's Blogger.com. Other examples of hosted blogging platforms include WordPress.com and MSN Spaces.

These platforms are referred to as hosted because they host your blog on their main domain. The URLs for blogs built on hosted platforms usually consist of the blog name and the platform's own URL. For example, if you built a blog named "myblog" on WordPress.com, your blog's URL would be www.myblog.wordpress.com. The wordpress.com extension shows that this blog is hosted on the www.wordpress.com domain instead of standing on its own.

Using a hosted blogging platform has a number of advantages. The first one, obviously, is that most hosted platforms are free. Building a blog on a hosted platform is also relatively easy. They usually come with a basic default template which allows you to set up your blog in a few minutes. Setting up usually involves choosing a template design and filling in a few fields. Anyone can use these platforms, even if you know nothing about the technological side of blogging. They are also very simple to run. They come with very user-friendly features that allow you to create your posts in almost the same way you would do on a word processor. Since they are targeted at beginners, hosted platforms automatically serve their updates. You do not have to upload any new software to the server. Instead, the updates happen seamlessly, sometimes even without your knowledge. Since they are hosted on established domains that already have good page ranks, blogs on hosted platforms are also indexed by such engines pretty quickly.

On the flip side, hosted blogging platforms have a number of disadvantages as well. The first is that they are less customizable than standalone platforms. With a hosted platform, you are stuck with the provided design templates and features. There is not much you can do if you want your blog to have a unique look or extended functionality. This results in many blogs looking very similar to each other. For instance, if you want to make any changes to the default blog templates in Blogger.com, you need to have HTML and CSSS skills.

With hosted platforms, you also have less control over your blog. While the content on your blog is your own, the blog is not technically yours since it is hosted on the platform's domain. This places you at the mercy of the platform, and there is not much you can do. For instance, if the platform's hosting has a problem, your blog might experience some down time, and there's not much you can do about that. The platform also has the right to shut down the blog if they feel that you are in violation of their terms.

I also mentioned that with a hosted platform, your blog URL will include the platform's URL. This robs your blog of much-needed memorability and professionalism. Sure, there are some successful blogs that are built on hosted platforms. However, it comes across as more professional when you have your own custom URL. Finally, upgrading from a hosted to a standalone platform can be much of a challenge. Actually, before you start on a hosted platform, it is good to consider what options you have in case your blog becomes big. Does the hosted platform allow you to easily move to a standalone platform? Remember, changing your domain will also affect some of your traffic, and you will have to start climbing the search engine ranking ladder all over again.

Hosted platforms are best suited for bloggers who do not really care about having their own unique domain and those who are not too concerned with customizing their blogs or adding some unique features. You should also keep in mind that many hosted platforms have strict regulations on how you can monetize your blog. For instance, many do not allow bloggers to serve ads on their blogs. For this reason, I do not recommend using a hosted blogging platform.

Standalone Blogging Platforms

Standalone blogging platforms allow you to host your blog under your own custom domain. The platforms simply provide a CMS for your online content. This is the most preferable option if you intend to build a professional blog. The most popular standalone blogging platform is Wordpress.org.

Using standalone blogging platforms has several advantages. First, it gives you full control over your blog's design. These platforms are very customizable. The only limit to what you can achieve with standalone blogging platforms is your web design skills. If you are not well-versed in web design, you can still use the default templates. Another advantage of standalone platforms is their adaptability. For instance, there is a huge army of developers who are constantly developing all manner of WordPress plugins. The plugins extend the functionality of the basic WordPress installation, allowing you to achieve and implement all kinds of things on your blog. Many other standalone platforms have their own communities of developers coming up with their own versions of plugins to extend the platforms' functionalities.

Another advantage is that most standalone platforms are free. Sure, you will be required to pay for your own domain name and hosting. However, access to the platform remains free. Finally, you get to have your own custom domain name. This makes your blog URL more memorable, makes your blog come across as more professional, and makes your blog easier to brand.

Despite these advantages, standalone blogging platforms are not without their downsides. First, they can be complicated to set up if you are not very technologically inclined. You will need to purchase your domain name and arrange for your own hosting. Some might require you to set up databases, download the platform to your computer and then upload all the files to your hosting server via FTP (File Transfer Protocol). However, many have tutorials that can help you with this process. Additionally, many web hosts are now installing these platforms for their users, making the process almost as simple as using a hosted platform.

Another disadvantage of standalone platforms is that you will have to bear the cost of your domain name (a one-off registration fee and a yearly renewal fee) as well as the hosting fee (renewed yearly). Luckily, these costs are not very high. When starting, you can get domain name and hosting packages for less than $50 a year. However, you might need to switch to a more expensive plan as your blog grows. Updating your platform's version can also be complicated, though most web hosts nowadays have in place systems for automatically installing updates.

Standalone blogging platforms are the best choice for bloggers who want to have their own custom URL and those who want the freedom to customize their blogs as they wish. With a standalone platform, you can configure your blog to look and work very professionally. The only limitation is your imagination and your skills. With standalone platforms, no one has control over your blog, so you can monetize it as you please. I recommend going the standalone route if your intention is to build a professional blog that you will use to earn a living.

With the above knowledge, you should be able to choose the best blogging platform for your needs. In my experience, the best blogging platform is WordPress.org, and I recommend that you use it. It is the most popular blogging platform, powering over 27% of all blogs and websites on the internet. Some reasons behind its popularity are:

> ➤ It is free to use (though you have to pay for your domain name and hosting).
> ➤ Setting up your blog on WordPress.org is quite easy.

➢ It has been around for a while and has proven its robustness and security.

➢ It is supported by a whole industry of developers, designers, and tool providers, helping users achieve more from the platform.

If you choose to build your blog on WordPress, keep in mind that there are two versions of WordPress:

WordPress.com: This is a hosted platform that you can start using without having to pay for anything. Your blog is hosted on the www.wordpress.com domain. You have less control over your blog's design and there are restrictions on the features that you can add and how you monetize your blog.

WordPress.org: This is a standalone platform that gives you control over your blog. Getting a domain name and hosting is up to you. There are no restrictions over how you use or monetize your blog. This is the best option. I am going to use WordPress.org in my explanations.

Getting A Domain Name and Setting Up Your Hosting

Now that you know the blogging platform you are going to use, it is time to pay for your domain name. We already discussed the process of choosing a domain name, so I won't touch on that. There are several places where you can pay for your domain name. Some good examples include

GoDaddy, HostGator, SiteGround, BlueHost, and NameCheap. Visit any of these domain registrars and enter your chosen domain name. If it available, you can go ahead and pay for it.

The next thing is to set up your hosting. It is advisable to have your blog hosted by the same company from which you have purchased your domain name. Once you pay for the hosting, the web host will guide you on how to set up your hosting. Setting up your hosting is a simple process that should not take you more than a few minutes.

Setting Up Your Blog

Once you are done setting up your domain and hosting, the next step is to install WordPress on your blog. Most web hosts have automated the process of installing WordPress, therefore this step should be super easy. You simply need to log into your web host account and find the "Install WordPress" button. Depending on your web host, you might need to select the "do it yourself (FREE)" version. From there, click on the "Install" button. You will be required to enter your domain. After you click on the "Check Domain" button, you will be required to accept the terms and conditions. Click on the checkbox next to the terms and conditions and press the "Install Now" button.

That's all. Once you do that, your blog is up. You can now proclaim to the world that you are a blogger. However, at this point, your blog still looks bland, so you need to make it look much better by installing a theme. WordPress has lots of free themes that you can install on your blog. You can also opt for paid themes if none of the free ones are to your liking.

That's it. Your blog is up and ready. You can now start working on posting your first piece of content.

Pay Per Click Advertising and Search Engine Optimization

If you're looking to drive more traffic to your website, then you've probably heard of the terms "pay per click advertising" and "search engine optimization" or "SEO." But what's the difference? And how does pay per click advertising (or PPC advertising) differ from search engine marketing or paid search?

Well, search engine marketing and paid search are just euphemisms for pay per click advertising, which is also known as PPC advertising, or Google advertising because the majority of pay per click advertising runs on the Google search network, Google content network, and Google display network.

When you hear "pay per click advertising," think advertising. The listings generated from pay per click advertising are paid for, and they appear in the "sponsored links" sections at the very top and far right-hand side of search results pages. They can also appear on other websites that "lease" space to Google and other search engines to display advertising.

The words "pay per click" in the term pay per click advertising also tell us something. With pay per click advertising, the website owner pays a specific amount each time a user clicks on their ad. In other words, they pay per click, hence the name "pay per click advertising."

Pay per click advertising can be useful for advertisers who require highly-predictable marketing budgets. That's because pay per click advertisers control precisely how much they're willing to spend on their pay per click advertising. In fact, you can set a daily budget to ensure you never spend more than your company can afford.

Something else to consider about pay per click advertising is that each time an ad appears and a user doesn't click on it, there's no cost. Therefore, a pay per click advertising listing can appear thousands of times, be seen by thousands of internet users, and as long as no one clicks on it, the advertiser doesn't have to pay.

Of course, the goal of pay per click advertising is for users to click on ads, but it's helpful to know pay per click advertising can increase visibility even when users aren't clicking. This is especially useful when pay per click advertisers use banner ads, which are graphically-designed display ads that serve to internet users based on their search behavior.

By comparison to pay per click advertising, search engine optimization (SEO) is not advertising at all. Unlike pay per click advertising, SEO relies on your website's content, programming, and back-links to increase the likelihood your listing will appear among the top search results. But just because search engine optimization is not advertising, don't think SEO is free. In fact, an SEO program can cost as much or more than pay per click advertising. That's because effective SEO requires hiring an expert to modify your website's content and coding. In addition, effective SEO programs require generating content and disseminating that content across the internet -- always with links back to your website. And all of this takes time and money.

On a more positive note, sophisticated internet users may be more likely to click on organic search results than on listings generated by pay per click advertising. The organic search results are listed below pay per click advertising results, and some internet users perceive these listings as more credible than pay per click advertising results.

Bottom line, both pay per click advertising and SEO are valuable and both should be part of your online marketing program. So if you want to increase visibility and traffic, make sure to set an adequate budget for pay per click advertising and SEO.

A website is the cheapest storefront you can ever purchase for your business. You do not have to pay rent and everything - from the cost of staff to the cost of inventory - is a fraction of what traditional businesses pay. But a storefront on the web does not mean much unless you have customers walking through your metaphorical front door. The quickest way to drive customers through the front door is pay per click advertising (also known as PPC). PPC places ads for your products and services on search engines like Google and social outlets like Facebook. When considering PPC for your business you have two options: go it alone and manage your own pay per click advertising campaign, or hire a pay per click advertising service. Neither one is an easy walk in the park.

Going It Alone

Pay per click can seem daunting for the uninitiated. Any business owner investigating the wilds of PPC for the first time will be confronted with the alphabet soup of terminology from Hell. "Bid management", "CPC", "Click Through Rate", "Keyword Planning", "Negative Keywords", and on and on and on. They will also find themselves in a thicket of terms of service and quality requirements. Google, for instance, has certain policies for each ad that must be abided by, or your ads will not be displayed.

Sound complicated? Yeah, because it is complicated. There is a reason that since the birth of PPC in the mid-2000s there has also been an accompanying explosion in pay per click advertising services that manage ad accounts. These pay per click management companies take the stress and time out of managing pay per click campaigns.

But not all pay per click advertising services are made of the same stuff. When looking at PPC Management companies you have a lot of choices. And picking the right type of management company will keep your business out of the woods.

PPC Management

PPC management agencies do exactly what the name implies; they manage your pay per click account for a percentage or a flat fee. Most often these agencies specialize in management for Google Adwords. In fact, Google encourages people to use agencies. They provide a Google Partners program where Adwords agencies can receive special benefits, like seminars and discounts.

Using pay per click advertising services for your business' website is a no-brainer. The brain-work comes into finding the right PPC management company for your company. There are several things to consider. What kind of service do they offer? Do they manage just Adwords or do they also handle other PPC channels, like Facebook and Bing? What is their reporting like? Do they provide weekly, bi-weekly, or monthly reports?

The chief thing to look for in any marketing agency is how they respond to and treat you as a customer. Think of your PPC management company in the same way you think of your stockbroker. If you have a significant amount of money at a stock brokerage you would expect to call and talk to your broker every week. You should expect that same level of service from your pay per click management company.

Pay per click advertising is the quickest way to drive traffic and business to your website. The key to effective PPC is not getting lost in the weeds and in most cases, that means using an agency to manage your pay per click campaign efforts. Still looking? Well, call us and we'll discuss how we can help you take advantage of your PPC campaign.

.

Don't try to go it alone. Find a company that can help you maximize you pay per click advertising

Creating A Content Strategy for Your Blog

You are going to learn how to create a solid content strategy for your newly created blog.

Let's face it, content is the core of your blog. You cannot be a blogger if you cannot produce content. Unfortunately, creating great content consistently is one of the hardest parts of blogging. One of the major mistakes many beginners make is starting a blog without any plan on how they will create content for it. If you do this, many are the days you will stare at a blank page wondering what you should write about. On the other hand, if you have a content strategy, you will have a good idea of what you audience wants to read about and when you need to put up which post.

Having a content strategy is what separates successful bloggers from the rest of the pack. With a content strategy, you won't waste hours creating content that no one cares about or trying to figure out what topic you need to cover next. A study by the Content Marketing Institute reported only 32% of bloggers without a content strategy are effective, compared to 60% of those who have a written content strategy. I am going to share seven steps which you can follow to come up with a good content strategy for your blog.

Step 1: Define Your Goals

This is the most important step in creating a content strategy. If you know not where you are going, you will not get there. Without clearly defined goals, the rest of the steps do not really matter. Therefore, take the time to define you blogging goals. What do you want to achieve with your blog? Is your goal to drive customers to your offline business? Is it to create awareness about your services? Is it to generate leads or increase sales? Are you trying to build a brand? Decide on two or three objectives that you want to achieve with your blog. Do not choose more than three objectives. If you do that, your blog will have no central focus, and your chances of achieving success will be greatly diminished.

When defining your goals, be very specific. Simply saying that you want to "generate more leads" for your business is not enough. You need to decide how may leads you want to generate and the timeframe in which you want to do it. In this case, a better goal would be "generate 30% more leads within the next four months". This goal is more specific, is time bound, and is measurable. With such a goal, it becomes easier to determine the kind of content you need to create, the number of people you need to reach, and so on.

Once you have defined your goals, you should then divide them into smaller targets or milestones that you can work towards in the short term. It is easier to follow through when you have small actions that you can take each day. Sometimes, you might need to change your goals. However, this should be done after you have achieved your current goals.

Step 2: Define Your Ideal Audience

Once you have defined your goals, the next step is to define your ideal target audience. Knowing who you are targeting allows you to create content that appeals to them. Your content will hardly be relevant if you do not know who you are writing for. Knowing who you are writing for also makes it easier for you to promote your content to these people. Many beginners make the mistake of assuming that they know their audience.

Knowing your audience goes beyond knowing that you are writing for motor enthusiasts, bikers, fitness enthusiasts, foodies, or pet owners. Knowing your readers involves knowing who they are, where thy hang out online, and what their likes and dislikes are. It involves knowing their needs, their desires, their frustrations, their fears, and what they are trying to achieve.

According to Henneke, a prominent business writing coach, you should treat your ideal audience like an imaginary friend. You should be able to hold a conversation with them the way you do with your close friends. You should be able to tell what gives them joy and what irks them. You should know the questions on their minds before they ask them. Only this way will you be able to connect with them.

When you know your audience's frustrations, challenges, and what they are trying to achieve, it becomes easier to create content that helps them get there. For instance, let's assume that you are a fitness blogger. Different people have different fitness goals. Some could be trying to lose weight, while others could be trying to gain muscle. It is impossible to create content that is relevant to both these two groups. However, if you know that your audience is comprised of the people trying to gain muscle, you can create content that is specifically geared toward helping them do that. This is what it means to know your audience. When starting your blog, you should be very specific about the audience you choose to focus on. Once you smash your goals for this audience, you can then add another similar audience.

Step 3: Come Up with Topic Ideas and Keywords

Now that you know who you are writing for, the next step is to find out what kind of content they like reading and some good keywords you want your content to rank for. When you have some ideas for a number of posts, you will be more organized, and more importantly, you will eliminate the not-so-uncommon sessions of staring at a blank screen wondering what you should write. So, how do you identify keywords and come up with topic ideas?

The first step is keyword research. When most people hear about keyword research, they think it involves entering a phrase they think is relevant and finding other related keywords. This is the wrong approach to keyword research. Your keyword research should be more strategic. Ideally, you want to find the best ranking topics that your readers would be interested in reading.

A good way of doing this is to find a competing blog that is both popular and trustworthy. Enter a link to this blog in the Google Keyword Planner tool and you will get a list of their top-ranking keywords, as well as related keywords that are highly searched for and read. Enter these keywords on Google to find the top-ranking articles for these keywords. Go through these articles to find out what they have in common that makes them successful. In addition, go through the comments and find out what information people are looking for that was missing from these articles.

Another way of finding content that your audience will love is to identify content that is already performing well. You can do this through Buzzsumo. This tool will show you the top performing content for your keywords, as well as the number of shares the content has received. You can also go to Quora and find the most common questions asked by users within your niche or around the keywords you identified. This will give you a general idea of the things that your audience might be interested in learning about. You can also look at some of the best performing posts by your competitors to give you ideas on the hottest topics within your niche.

Step 4: Design Content That Will Get You and Your Audience Closer to Your Goals

Now that you have identified some topics that your audience would love to learn about, it's time to come up with a content plan that will move your audience from where they are (what they are struggling with) to where they want to be (what they want to achieve). The same content will also take you to your goals.

Your content acts as a conveyor belt for your audience by moving them through the following stages:

Awareness – Research – Comparison/Validation – Purchase

Similarly, your content conveyor belt will move you closer to your goals by moving your audience through the following stages:

Stranger – Reader – Subscriber – Loyal Fan – Customer

To effectively move your audience from one phase to another, you need to understand what keeps them stuck in each phase and how your content can help them overcome this obstacle. The content you publish should not merely be treated as content. Instead, you should think of your content as a catalyst that spurs people to achieve specific results. This means that every piece of content you post should have a specific purpose. You will only achieve results with your blogging if you match your content to where your audience members are on their journey.

Look at the blog post ideas you came up with and identify which step of your audience's journey they match. Organize these topics in such a way that they will help move your audience through the various stages.

Step 5: Determine the Best Format for Your Content

When people think of blogging, they automatically think of serving their content as written posts. However, have you considered whether your audience might have greater preference for other content formats? Apart from text, you can also serve your content as audio, video, or even as presentations or live webinars.

Apart from the actual medium of content presentation, there are other considerations that you also need to keep in mind. Does your ideal audience prefer short posts or longer, more detailed ones? Have you thought of incorporating images in your posts? Have you thought of incorporating listicles and case studies as part of your content? All these have an impact on the ability of your content to reach your ideal audience.

So, how do you decide which format is best for your blog? Again, you can glean this information from your competitors. Look at your competitors' blogs and try to find out the content formats that their audiences are most receptive to. Go through the comments on their blog posts and look for clues as to the kind of content their followers are most interested in. Once you have built a significant readership, you can also post a survey to your readers asking them what their preferences are. You can also visit forums within your niche to find out the kind of content the members are sharing. All these strategies will help you come up with the correct content profile to help you grow your blog.

Step 6: Create an Editorial Calendar

Another major mistake most beginners make is to post randomly on their blogs. The problem with this is that you tend to lose focus and prioritize other things over your blog. To prevent this, you need to create an editorial calendar. This is a posting schedule detailing when you will post and which post needs to be posted on which day. An editorial calendar helps you keep yourself on track and ensures that all your posts are published on time.

Since you have already come up with a list of (hopefully 15 to 20) blog post ideas and decided the order in which you are going to post them, all that is left is to decide when each post will be published. When coming up with an editorial calendar, you should consider your lifestyle. Don't come up with a schedule that you know will be difficult for you to follow. Instead, go for one that allows you to remain consistent. For instance, posting an article every day might sound awesome, but can you really manage that? Will you even have enough time to promote each post?

I would recommend working with a posting schedule of two to four posts every month. This gives you enough time to come up with high-quality posts, as well as to promote your posts every time you publish. With a schedule of two posts per month, the 15 to 20 post ideas you came up with will take you through seven to 10 months, which is enough time to build a decent amount of traffic. Whatever posting schedule you settle on, make sure that it is workable for you, and ensure that you stick to it.

There are several tools that you can use for your editorial calendar. A good editorial calendar should be able to give you a bird's eye view of your posting schedule. It shows you all the planned posts, when each post is due and the stage of the audience journey that it is targeted for. If there are people helping you to create content, your editorial calendar should also be able to give you visibility into who is working on which piece of content. Some free tools you can use to create your editorial calendar include Google Calendar or Trello. If you are looking for a more dedicated calendar

with an extended set of features, you can check out
CoSchedule.

Step 7: Create Amazing Content

You have defined your goals, you thoroughly know
and understand your ideal audience, you have done your
keyword research, you have your topics, and you have
created your content calendar. Now is time to go ahead and
create amazing content for your audience.

There are a number of things that separate great
content from ordinary, run-of-the-mill content. Great
content is well written, with correct spelling and grammar
and with simple language that is easy to understand. It is well
researched and makes use of examples, case studies, and
useful stats. It utilizes media to help your audience grasp the
concepts better. Finally, great content is properly formatted
for easy readability.

It might be tempting to create and publish content
randomly as it comes to mind. However, having a clear
content strategy will save you hours of time and lots of
headache. You will also be more effective when you follow a
content strategy. You will be better prepared and your
blogging career will be a lot more fun when you know what
you are supposed to be doing instead of stumbling in the
dark. The best part is that coming up with a good content
strategy only takes a few hours.

Building Traffic

You are going to learn how to attract traffic and build an audience for your blog.

Making money from blogging involves two things: building an audience and then selling them something. Now that you have set up your blog and written a few pieces of content, it is time to find readers. The mistake most new bloggers make is that they create great content, share it with their friends on their social media pages, and wait for a ton of traffic to flood to their blog. Sadly, this never happens, and many of them give up as a result. You need to understand that creating great content is only half the battle. You also need to aggressively promote your content. As the popular saying in blogging circles goes, content might be king, but promotion is queen.

So, how do you get people to start reading your blog posts? Below are some tried and tested techniques that are guaranteed to grow your blog's traffic over time.

Offer Valuable Content

I mentioned that you should make sure you create great content. I will reiterate this because it is crucial to building an audience for your blog. You should make sure that the posts on your blog provide your readers with meaningful and useful information that is relevant to their lives. Remember, people are on your blog because they want to learn something new, solve a problem, or achieve their goals. Your blog posts should help them do that.

Unfortunately, most new bloggers do not do this. They take the same content that is on a hundred other blogs and rehash it. If your content is the same as the content on a hundred other blogs, why should I bother reading it? Find a way to create content that is unique to your blog. Avoid plagiarizing content from other bloggers. Instead, take trending topics within your industry and dissect them in your own personal voice. Experiment with different types of content formats and find out what works best.

Consistency

The second most important thing you should keep in mind is keeping your blog regularly and consistently updated. The posting frequency is not really a huge concern. You can decide on a posting schedule that works best for you, whether that is daily, weekly, or monthly. Once you decide on a certain posting schedule, make sure you follow it religiously. If you post inconsistently or decrease your posting frequency for some reason, your traffic is going to take a hit. The worst part about this is that to overturn the decline in traffic resulting from one month of inconsistency, you will need several months of consistent posting.

SEO

Search engines are a major source of traffic; therefore, it is important for you to make sure that potential readers can find your blog and your posts on search engines. Every single day, people perform over seven billion searches on Google. By optimizing your blog and posts for search engines, you can direct some portion of this massive traffic to your blog. SEO is a complex and multi-faceted element. However, there are some easy SEO strategies that will go a long way in driving traffic to your blog. One of these is doing proper keyword research and ensuring that you include these keywords in your blog post content, title, and Meta descriptions. If your post contains images, include the keywords as part of the image name instead of using generic names like "kdhfk.jpg". You should also include relevant tags in your posts. There are some free WordPress plugins you can use to automate your blog's SEO, such as the Yoast Wordpress SEO plugin.

Blog Commenting

Blog commenting involves reading posts and leaving comments on the posts, with a link back to your blog. Blog commenting does two things. First, it is a great way of establishing relationships with other bloggers in your niche. Second, leaving relevant comments on posts by high-authority bloggers can send lots of traffic to your blog. To implement this technique, come up with a list of the most relevant blogs in your niche. Regularly read the posts on these blogs, leave comments, and interact with other people commenting on these blogs. Do not leave one-line comments that do not add value to the posts. Instead, write detailed comments that add information to the post or that answer questions posed by other commenters. If you do it regularly, the other bloggers and their visitors will soon notice your expertise in your field and some of them will definitely visit your blog. Depending on the kind of comments you leave, you might even get a chance to guest post on these top blogs, something that can drive huge traffic to your blog.

Article Marketing

This is another easy technique that can drive lots of traffic to your blog if it is done properly. This technique involves creating short articles within your niche and distributing them to free article marketplaces. These articles are a great way to showcase your expertise in your industry. These articles are usually accompanied by an author by-line that consists of your bio and a link back to your blog, giving you the chance to tell people about yourself and to direct them to your blog. Since these articles will be distributed all over the internet, they help you to reach audiences that you would have been unable to reach through other means.

Guest Blogging

This is one of the best and the most effective ways of growing traffic to your blog. Guest blogging essentially involves tapping into the traffic of established bloggers in your niche who have more traffic than you. Guest blogging helps you showcase your expertise, lets people interested in your niche know about your blog, and drives some of these people to your blog. The backlinks generated from guest posting also contribute to your SEO. To implement this technique, make a list of successful blogs with a huge and engaged audience within your niche. Reach out to the owners of these blogs and pitch your guest post ideas. Make sure to show them how they will benefit from your guest post. Once they agree to your pitch, go ahead and create a unique and high-quality post. Once the post is up on their blog, promote it the same way you promote posts on your own blog. Make sure to engage with readers who comment on the post and respond to their questions.

Invite Other Bloggers to Guest Post on Your Blog

This is the inverse of the previous technique. Instead of reaching out to top bloggers within your niche with the aim of writing guest posts on their blogs, pitch to them the idea of them writing a guest post on your blog. Once the post is live, there is a high likelihood that they will promote it to their audience, bringing loads of traffic to your blog. If you have more amazing content on your blog, some of their audience might also end up becoming loyal fans of your blog.

Social Media

Today, almost every person with access to the internet is active on one social media platform or another. You can take advantage of all these users to drive traffic to your blog. Create social media profiles for your blog on the platforms where your target audience are most likely to be found. These include sites like Facebook, Instagram, Twitter, Pinterest, Google+, Tumblr, and LinkedIn. With its over 2.2 billion active users, Facebook is my favorite. However, do not restrict yourself to Facebook. Every time you put up a new post, share it on your social media profiles. Once you create a habit of regularly sharing great content on your social media profiles, this can easily become your biggest source of traffic.

Here are some strategies you can use to get more results from social media:

Share your content severally: Once you put up a post on your blog, share it on all the platforms on which you are active. Customize each update for its specific platform. For instance, you can include hashtags when posting on Instagram and Twitter, though this wouldn't work on Facebook. You should also share these updates a couple of times on each platform, with a few days or weeks between each update.

Ride on new social features: When social media platforms launch new features, these features attract a lot of attention. Good examples of these are Twitter moments and Instagram stories. You can ride on the popularity of these new features to drive more traffic to your blog.

Each update should be unique: While I said that you should share each post a couple of times on social media, the updates should not be identical. Change the caption every time you share it to appeal to a wider audience.

Forums

Another great source of traffic is online forums. Forums are places where people interested in a topic meet to discuss matters related to the topic. The top forums in most niches usually have hundreds of thousands of members. They are also visited by millions of people each month. You can take advantage of forums to drive some of this traffic to your blog. However, to do this, you need to have the right approach. Do not simply start posting links to your blog in every post on the forum. This is seen as being spammy and might even get you kicked out of the forum. Instead, after joining the forum, take some time to learn how it operates. Interact with other members by contributing to discussions and answering the questions posed by other members. Do this for a while before you start sharing links to your blog. Once you start sharing links, use your forum signature. Since the members have already seen you and your contributions on the forum, many of them are going to click through to your blog.

Influencer Marketing

Sometimes, you will come across blogs that seem to come out of nowhere, and in a very short time, they are among the top blogs in that niche and are considered as thought leaders in their industries. How do they achieve this in such a short time? In most cases, the bloggers behind them take advantage of the power of influencer marketing. Rather than following the slow and steady route of building an audience by consistently sharing their content on social media for a long time, they take a short cut by connecting with industry movers and shakers. Influencer marketing involves reaching out to reputable figures within your industry and having them share your content. Since these figures are already known and trusted within your niche, sharing your content is seen as an endorsement for your blog. Their huge following will flock to your blog. This is one of the quickest ways of growing your audience and building your blog's authority.

Content Repurposing

Most bloggers confine themselves to written content. The problem with this is that by doing so, you confine yourself to a small portion of your potential audience. Some people might not be huge fans of reading online content, but maybe they enjoy watching video content. By converting your content into multiple formats, you are able to reach a wider audience. For example, after creating a blog post, you can record a video of yourself discussing the information shared in the blog post and share the video on YouTube. You can then share an audio version of the video as a podcast. You can compress the information from your blog post into a slide deck and post it on SlideShare. You can design the slide deck into a magazine and post it on FlipBoard. If you do all this, you will reach five different audiences from five different platforms, whereas you would have only reached a single audience of you stopped at creating a blog post.

One thing you should consider is posting on these other platforms in addition to your blog. You should also link back to your blog from these other platforms. This way, you have a chance of converting your inbound links to customers. For example, on youtube, if you do not link to your blog, someone will watch your video on YouTube and then move on to other videos. That is a lost opportunity.

Optimize Your Content for Clicks and Shares

To increase the traffic on your blog, you also need to ensure that your content is optimized to get more social media shares and repeat visits. How do you do this? First, you should ensure that most of your posts are based on evergreen content. Evergreen content is content that is relevant all year round, and even a couple of years down the line. Sure, you can get lots of initial traffic from seasonal posts, trending topics, and breaking news. However, evergreen content drives more traffic in the long run. Since it will be relevant even a year after you post it, it is also likely to receive shares for much longer.

Another technique to optimize your content for more clicks is to serialize your blog posts. This means that you should create a series of continuous posts. By dangling subsequent parts of your series in front of your readers, you can increase your email subscriptions. Serialized posts are usually comprehensive and very valuable. Therefore, even if you do not use them to drive email subscriptions, your visitors are likely to share these posts and check back on them severally as they try to solve their problem.

Email List Building

This is one of the most reliable sources of traffic for bloggers. It is also one of the most effective tools for converting visitors into customers. Sadly, this is something that is often ignored by newbie bloggers. If you want to get ahead of the pack, you should start building your email list immediately after launching your new blog (of course you should have at least a preliminary list before your blog launch so you can start building buzz, but don't worry if the list isn't huge, you can build up from anywhere). Why is email so effective? With the increasing dependence on mobile devices, more and more people are reading their emails on mobile. Therefore, through email, you can reach your audience at any time of the day, regardless of where they are. Every time you put up a new post on your blog, share it with your subscribers via email. People who have taken the liberty to subscribe to your email list have already demonstrated that they are interested in your content. Therefore, they are more likely to click through to your post. They are also more likely to comment on your posts and share them with their followers on social media. Research has shown that email subscribers share content 3.9 times more than other visitors.

Partnerships

You can also drive free traffic to your blog by getting into partnerships with other bloggers within your niche. There are several blog networks out there. All you need to do is to identify and become a member of the most relevant ones in your niche. Apart from joining blog networks and blogger Facebook groups, you should reach out to other bloggers within your niche and form partnerships where each of you promotes the other's posts to your respective audiences. This means that you should continuously try to connect with other top bloggers in your niche. Some of them won't accept your request, and that is fine. However, if you have something to bring to the table, many will accept, and both of you will be able to increase traffic to your blogs.

Please note that while this sounds like a great way to increase traffic and work together with other bloggers, you need to make sure whatever content you're promoting is relevant to your brand and your audience. Your audience will get annoyed if you keep promoting the content of other bloggers if they don't find it helpful or interesting. Blog readers don't want to be aggressively "promoted at," they want to be informed and entertained. Always keep this in mind when considering strategies to increase traffic or generate more content. Your first priority should always be keeping your readers happy.

Run Contests

When you have just launched a new blog, it is very important to create some buzz around it. There is no better way of doing this than giving people an incentive for visiting your blog. This is where contests come in. Contests require visitors to engage with your blog in some way (commenting, sharing your posts, or subscribing to your emails) in order to be eligible to receive some prizes. Find something that you can give out and promote your contest on social media. People love free things, and they are definitely going to check out and engage with your blog if that means the possibility of winning a prize.

Incidentally, this is also a good way to build an email list and generate likes, shares and comments on Facebook. If you offer a giveaway or contest, people will be willing to share your content. Although they may not become lifelong followers, it may help your content to become more visible and it may even go viral if you get enough traffic.

Budget for Ads

The methods mentioned so far are free methods of driving traffic to your blog. However, if you want to see faster results and if you have the money to spend, you should put up paid ads on your blog's social media channels. Most social media platforms have a way of determining what their users see on their timelines. However, through targeted ads, you can reach a more targeted audience that is relevant to your niche. Facebook is a particularly great platform for paid ads since it has excellent targeting and a wide reach. You do not have to pay for ads every single day. However, with a relatively small budget, you can drive lots of traffic to your blog through paid ads.

Watch Your Analytics

It is of no use to drive traffic to your blog if you do not keep track of your traffic statistics. You can keep track of your blog's traffic statistics through your site's built-in statistics or through free apps like Google Analytics. Discover which posts are most popular and identify the common factor between them. Try to replicate this in your other posts. Analytics will also show you where most of your traffic is coming from. You can then focus your efforts on those platforms. If you find that some other blogs are driving traffic to your blog, reach out to them and thank them for promoting your content. You can also point them to some other relevant posts that they might have overlooked. Without tracking your traffic and engagement metrics, it will be very difficult to determine what works and what you need to improve.

Section 2: Affiliate Marketing

What Is Affiliate Marketing?

Affiliate marketing has become popular over the years. It is estimated that the affiliate marketing industry in the United States is worth nearly $5 billion a year and brands in the United Kingdom are worth £1 billion. In addition, more than three-quarters of brands use some form of affiliate marketing to promote their products.

The types of businesses that are utilizing affiliate marketing are diverse in nature. You will find health care product companies, travel agencies, fashion brands, and many others working with these campaigns. Practically any business in the world can start using affiliate marketing if enough ideas are produced.

What is affiliate marketing and what makes it such a popular option for making money? This chapter is about what makes this practice unique and noteworthy. Affiliate marketing is a practice where a person promotes a business and receives money from that business for each sale or referral. It is a simple way of making money online.

This is a growing market and much of its popularity is due to how the process works, and how it makes it easier for people to promote what they are offering to others in a simple and easy-to-follow way.

The Main Definition

Affiliate marketing is a practice that can take many

forms although it is particularly popular online. With this form of marketing, a business will entrust its promotional efforts to others. This practice works with a simple setup. A company allows people who sign up as marketers to promote their business and/or products. A company will offer particular referral codes and promotional materials to those marketers.

A marketer then offers the products and/or materials online. This can be done on a personalized website or blog, among other places. The key is that these promotional materials have to be visible. Visitors to a site will then click on a link that the affiliate has posted online. The visitor must reach a site through that particular link before the affiliate can be paid anything.

Affiliates will receive a small cut of the sales that are driven by their work. The total will vary based on where the affiliate goes for the campaign. If the campaign works well, it can be a great way to earn money.

Why Is This Useful for a Business?

Affiliate marketing is a way to make money from home that can benefit anyone. It is a simple process that helps merchants to get their products and services out to a larger audience. It also allows merchants to keep the pressure of marketing from being too intense. This occurs because companies are allowing the public to market their wares.

By letting affiliates market products, a merchant can more easily focus on production, rather than marketing. This can also give a brand the opportunity to be promoted in a variety of ways. While any company could put up web advertisements or even promote itself on television, sometimes those messages become too repetitive. They can get so old that they will lose their meaning. For instance, all those ads for car insurance that you watch on television could become so repetitive that you no longer really care that a particular insurance provider might promise you better deals on a policy.

However, with affiliate marketing, a business can be promoted with a greater variety of messages. Each affiliate could market a product with his or her own particular messages. These might involve reviews, demonstrations, or news stories about whatever is available.

A business will appreciate the affiliate marketing process as it allows the marketing to be a little more exciting. Use your own creativity and consider many ideas you might have to promote a product or company.

The Main Players

There are several people who must work together to make any affiliate marketing campaign effective. These people are the following:

The Merchant

The merchant is the business responsible for starting up the affiliate marketing campaign. The merchant may also be called the business, retailer, advertiser, or brand. The merchant sells a certain product or service. It could sell tangible products for use in the home or business. It could also sell travel services, financial solutions, broadband online access, or anything else that people spend money on. A merchant must initiate a campaign. The merchant will set up the rules about how the campaign is to be run and how people are to be compensated.

The Network

While you can find many merchants with whom to do business, you need to contact a merchant through a particular network. This is to make it easier for you to find something available for your use. The network is the grouping that offers an affiliate program in which people can participate. The party who wants to be an affiliate will have to prepare a reasonable campaign and list it on the network site.

When the affiliate finds the marketing opportunity, the network will send information to the merchant regarding who has signed up. The merchant then sends out the proper marketing materials for the task at hand. The network also helps with managing the payments that take place during the campaign. It reviews how well affiliates work and delivers money based on what an affiliate can do.

A network will also receive some of the profits from each sale. These are not necessarily worth as much as what the affiliate or the merchant will receive but can still be worthwhile. In some cases, the network might provide the merchant with templates for the marketing materials to be utilized. Such templates can vary according to each network but they should be easy to customize and then implement. You do not always have to go through a network when finding a marketing campaign but it does help to at least get the support of one.

The Affiliate

Your role in the chain is as an affiliate. It is your work that is vital to the success of any marketing effort. The affiliate is the person who is responsible for getting the word out on whatever the merchant is offering. The affiliate will sign up with the merchant's plan through a network.

The affiliate can be anyone. It could be a blogger, a website operator, or a social media maven. Whatever the case, the affiliate should be someone who can get around online and interact with people in many ways. This person will accept information about all the materials that the merchant offers through the network. The affiliate will then have to manage the marketing items and use them properly as a means of potentially receiving a good payout.

In some cases, a separate manager can help with operating the affiliate program. This might entail working with a website or another method of promotion on a regular basis. Either way, monitoring and a lot of effort are required to ensure that the marketing process works well.

The Customer

The customer is the fourth and most important part of the affiliate marketing process. Without the customer, the campaign in question will fail. The marketing materials must reach the customer for the campaign to be successful. The affiliate must make sure such marketing items are appealing and useful in the eyes of the potential client. This ensures that the client will feel motivated and willing to become a customer.

With all four parties working together in the affiliate marketing process, it becomes easier for each of them to get what they want. Merchants can get the word out about their products and are more likely to make money. Networks can help with forwarding offers to the public and even participate in the profits. Affiliates will earn money from each referral that they produce. Finally, customers benefit by having access to information on a product or service that they are interested in and wish to purchase.

The customer is the key to ensuring that the marketing campaign works. Plenty of effort is needed by the other three parties to create messages and products or services that are worthwhile and of interest but in the end, it is up to the customer to decide if a transaction is made.

In particular:

      1. The merchant must have a useful product.

      2. The network must be able to establish a platform for the merchant to use.

3. The affiliate has to create a smart campaign that is unique and works to highlight what the merchant is selling.

The true magic happens when all three parties work together.

A General Layout for Bringing in Payouts

Here's how affiliate marketing works:

1. A merchant will contact a network to solicit help with producing a new campaign.

2. The network informs the merchant what promotional materials are needed.

3. The merchant configures the promotional materials with messages and images that fit whatever is being offered.

4. An affiliate signs up to work with the merchant to promote the products.

5. The affiliate will utilize the materials that he/she has received from the merchant to initiate a campaign designed by the affiliate.

6. A website, blog, or other places that list these advertisements or other messages are investigated and chosen by the affiliate. The affiliate will then program the marketing materials properly while consistently updating and controlling the materials.

7. A customer will click on a link or advertisement on such a website or blog.

8. The customer will have a cookie stored on the network's browser which indicates that he or she was referred to a site by the affiliate.

9. The customer purchases a product on the website to which he or she was led by the affiliate. The cookie that lists the referral information may be intact for a period of time.

10.   The affiliate will receive a portion of the sale that was produced. This is an amount or percentage predetermined by the merchant,

11.   The network also receives a portion of the sale.

This is a very simple layout to follow and provides a person with earnings from each sale that takes place. The process also shows just how important all four parties are in the process. All parties must work together to ensure that a transaction can be accomplished effectively.

What Can Be Promoted?

Practically anything can be promoted for sale through an affiliate marketing campaign. Some of the products and services you can promote online are listed below.

- The health care industry is a big driver of the affiliate marketing industry. People often promote prominent supplements, services, and health goods online.

- Books about all kinds of subjects are promoted online too. These include recipe books, weight loss guides, and even books on how to take care of specific types of pets.

- Computer software can be promoted through a campaign. You could use your campaign to highlight any kind of program that people could download or purchase online.

- Travel services are big in the affiliate marketing industry. These include services like air travel, hotel services, or booking solutions.

- Tech products are always being marketed online through affiliate programs. These tech products include tablets and smartphones, portable media players, television sets, and smart appliances.

- The auto industry can benefit from affiliate marketing too. Companies that make car products like floor mats, cargo materials, electronic adapters, assorted parts, tires, shocks, or brakes can look to affiliates to help get their campaigns off the ground.

There are no real limits on what people can promote through affiliate marketing campaigns. You have the option to market anything you want although the marketing options you have to work with will vary based on where you go to find them. Search diligently to see what you could utilize to find a campaign worth promoting.

How to Find Opportunities

It is easy to find affiliate marketing opportunities today. You can go online and find a program directory or a network website that lists information on what is available. You can also go directly to the website of a merchant who is running a program. You can get specific information on that site about what is available to use.

The options available to you when finding marketing campaigns are vast. Search to see what is open and you will surely find something that interests you. Check on a search engine to see what is out there.

How Are People Paid?

There are three particular ways that people can be paid in an affiliate marketing campaign. These vary based on what is being offered. The type of payment options that a merchant offers to affiliates should be analyzed based on the values, and how you can qualify to receive them:

1. Traditional Commissions

A traditional commission would simply be a percentage of the sale. For instance, you might get 50 or 60 percent of the sale that you generate by your referral. This is the most commonly utilized type of commission.

2. Cost-Per-Action

The cost-per-action option refers to a situation where a merchant pays the affiliate for each acquisition. For instance, a merchant might pay an affiliate for each click onto a site or for every time someone signs up for email messages. Merchants often use this for marketing because they know they do not have to pay for anything unless they can actually get people to buy or sign up for whatever they have to offer.

3. By-the-Product Sales

By-the-product sales refer to when very specific physical items are purchased from a site. Instead of being valued based on a percentage of the sale, your payment is a set amount based on the type of product you help sell. This often works in cases where large items for sale are being promoted. For instance, if you forwarded a person to a site that sells vacuum cleaners, you might receive a commission of $75 for each vacuum that a person buys from your link. This could work for any type of vacuum that qualifies for the sale.

These three options for getting paid are different but they can all be profitable. The amount of money you earn as an affiliate depends on the effort you put into the program.

Be certain you know what to expect in the way of payments when you get your campaign up and running. Additional information on how payments can be provided to you will be covered in a later chapter in this guide. This includes details on some special and intriguing ways to receive even more money.

How to Start an Affiliate Marketing Business

The possibilities for earning money are endless when you get an affiliate marketing business up and running. To make it all work, you must look at how you can start. You will have to do more than just find a business with which you might want to start as an affiliate. You must also look at what you will need to do to set up the affiliate program so you can get the most out of your work.

Much of this entails more than just finding a marketing campaign. You must also look at how you will set up a website and how you are going to keep it running. Ensuring everything is available and simple to follow makes it easier for you to market your work and make it viable.

A quick note: getting your marketing business up and running can take a while. You will have to spend weeks, if not months, getting your campaign ready. The goal is to ensure you put in the effort needed to make your affiliate site visible so people can actually use it. As you get more traffic onto your site, it becomes easier for you to make money. However, it does take effort to get that traffic; this is something that needs to be carefully considered.

You have the freedom to spend as much or as little time as you want to create an affiliate marketing campaign that works but you should still think carefully about what you could do. You're going to get more money and be more likely to succeed if you spend a greater amount of time getting your work ready.

Choose Your Niche

To start, look at the particular niche on which your campaign will focus. You should choose a niche that is interesting to you and is something to which you can stay connected. The key is to think about how you will work on your niche over time. You have to be developing something that you will actually want to work with for months or even years to come.

Just think about something that you have a strong interest in and search to see what is open on an affiliate network. It's always worth considering something you have studied for a while or have extensive knowledge of. Today you have many options to find something of interest. The niches that are available include such choices as the following:

- The health industry is huge as people are always looking to find ways to be happier with their bodies and to live longer.

- Travel services are popular as people love to travel the world and see new things.

- Parenting is an important niche as adults are always looking for ways to be better parents.

- The home and garden field cover many segments to which people devote a large amount of time and money. These include the fields of landscaping, tree maintenance, and weed control.

- Pets are always great to focus on as people spend a lot of money on their pets.

- The world of food is extensive as people are always finding ways to make new recipes and meals. Some aspects of food, particularly the wine industry, are a little more detailed and elaborate than others.

- Software and digital products are becoming a huge area for affiliate marketing as well. The advantage of these products is that you can often get a huge commission—I've seen them as high as 50% of the sale price of the software. If you promote someone's premium online course, and that course costs $2,000, you could get $1,000 of that just for referring them to the website.

Think about what interests you most when looking for affiliate marketing campaigns. You will have a better shot at succeeding if you choose a niche that is of strong interest to you. One of the reasons that so many people struggle to produce great affiliate marketing campaigns is that they do not enjoy the niches they have chosen. They may not be all that familiar with them and might have a tough time figuring out interesting bits of content to include.

By following a niche that you are actually interested in, you will have a better chance at making money. You will have more ideas and greater desire to work on something of value. All the work you put in will be worthwhile if you stick with an interesting niche that is useful and important to you.

Remember much of your endeavor will focus on explaining to people what makes your niche especially appealing.

Additional information on the niches that you could consider will be covered later in this book. This includes details on some of the more popular options that are available for you to pursue.

Review the Viability of Your Niche

Don't forget to see if the niche in question is viable. It should be one in which there is a strong potential for you to make a decent amount of money. Think about whether people will be interested in your niche five or ten years down the line. This might seem like a long time but it is important as it ensures your niche is something that will provide you with a viable chance to make money over time.

More importantly, you must think about how viable your interest in the niche will be. Is your niche something that you will continue to have a strong interest in years from now? If so, then it is a segment worth considering. You do not want to work on a site for months or years and then have it ruined because either the market has changed or you have lost interest or feel burned out.

Decide What to Write

As you choose your niche, decide what you would like to write about it. The odds are you will write dozens of blog posts or social media articles on whatever your niche might be. Try to come up with a decent variety of topics relating to your niche before you start. If you plan on working with a marketing campaign involving gardening, then you might consider writing articles about types of soil, aeration, preparing a garden bed for winter, weeding, and anything else relating to gardens.

The key is to come up with various good ideas relating to your niche. Think about what you can do and see if you could run a blog or website for months on end with new stories regularly posted. On a related note, look at whether new developments in your niche might be happening. This could be worthwhile if you are in the health sector as there are always discoveries and health advice to be written about. The tech sector is also popular as many new items are always being developed in today's tech world.

Review or Resource?

Most affiliate marketing sites work with one of two different models: a review model or a resource one. A review model is a layout where you could review products or services. You could discuss things relating to how something works and what makes it special. Let's say that you start a website that focuses on home remodeling tasks. You might talk about certain tools or machines that might help with completing specific tasks. One review might be about a paint stripper while another might be about a stud finder you could use on your walls.

A resource model focuses on explaining certain concepts. It is about some of the more specific or unique ideas that might find in your field. For a home remodeling resource site, you would include articles like tips on how to lay a new flooring surface or how to figure out where a new window or light should be installed.

These two kinds of website options are different from each other in terms of how they focus on particular things of value to you.

Be Specific

Although the niche you choose can cover many topics, you should be as specific as possible. For instance, you might consider a plan to market home improvement products on your site or you might want to focus on one specific aspect of home improvement.

You could produce a site that focuses on floor maintenance and installation. You can also have one about painting. Sticking with one very specific action is always worthwhile. This lets you focus on marketing your work and being distinctive in some way. Best of all, people will trust you because they know you focus on one very important part of your field. This, in turn, increases the chances of earning more pay through your marketing campaign.

Tips to Become a Successful Affiliate Marketer

Anyone can be a successful affiliate marketer.

However, not everyone knows what they can do to make a campaign stand out. There are a few smart tips that you must use if you wish to prepare a great affiliate marketing site that fits well and has a good layout that is easy to use.

Keep the Products or Services You Promote Connected

First, you should look at how the products or services you are promoting work with each other. See if they are connected in some way. An example of this might be a site that focuses on healthy living. You could market a website that sells fitness equipment and training machines. Meanwhile, you could also have an affiliation with a merchant that sells weight loss supplements or other nutritional products. Keeping these two types of products or sites together is perfect. The first site offers tools people can use to get in shape. The second includes things that improve upon the results of their weight loss or fitness routine. By combining products, you are producing a site where it is easy to connect products.

Always Be Honest

You might feel positive about some product or service you are highlighting on your site but what if you don't like a certain part of it? Honesty is the best policy. It is unclear who said that first but it is true. People like it when others are honest. They want to get the facts about something without filters. It's no wonder that so many people on both sides of the political aisle are frustrated with "fake news".

Your marketing site should be honest about

everything that is on it. Let the reader know what you do like about something but also talk about the negatives. Explain what you think could be improved upon or what can be done to keep those negatives from being too prevalent. Honesty builds trust in your site and lets people see that you care about their needs.

As you do this, be careful with how you are expressing your values. Do not go too far when talking about negative things. The last thing you want to do is make something look so negative that your target audience will not actually want to use it.

You can even include a note if you're posting content and articles saying something like, "Please note, I may receive a small affiliate commission if you use my link to purchase this product." Although this may turn some people off, it may encourage even more people to actually use the link you've provided instead of opening a new tab and googling the product or something. People often want to support small businesses and if they feel like you're providing them with quality information, they will be happy to support you if possible.

Be Realistic About Your Audience

Your audience is vital to the success of your program. You must carefully consider how you are treating your audience and that you understand what they are asking for. Think first about what your audience will actually buy. The analytics that you use for reviewing your audience should help you make good choices about what you will promote to your audience.

As you learn more about your audience, you should be realistic. Think about what the audience members would actually purchase. Would your clientele really be interested in something flashy or very expensive? Do you know and understand your customers' values? Do not assume that your audience members would be interested in just anything. Make sure you plan your sales offers properly and that you know what the readers will likely start asking for when they read your site.

What Will Your Readers Actually Spend?

This next point is vital when you are aiming to add new products onto your affiliate marketing site. You might notice that people are spending money to buy one item that is right on your site. Think about how much money that product costs as you look for new products to add.

As you find products, choose only those that you know your audience is willing to spend money on. Just because people are clicking on your links to buy a $25 e-book does not mean they would also click on something to buy a $300 appliance. Keeping the values of each product or service for sale consistent or close to one another is always best. This requires understanding of your audience and enough analytics to see how well your sales are running. When used properly, this strategy allows your site to grow and be marketable.

When Will People Buy Your Products?

The promotional work that you add to your site

should reflect the season. Do not try to market products that are obviously out of season. Sometimes the window of opportunity for promoting something is rather large. Let's say that you have an affiliate campaign with an airline that offers travel packages to many popular destinations. You might consider posting information on specials a few months before those events take place. This would give the reader enough time to plan a trip and reserve a flight through one of your links.

In other cases, the window might be a little tighter. For example, you might have a plan to promote lawn care and landscaping products. During the winter season, you would have to talk about things that can be done to prevent frost and other winter-related conditions from impacting a yard or landscape. Meanwhile, you could talk about watering tools during the summer or aeration items in the spring or another time when people might be planting gardens.

The timing of anything you post is vital. Think about how much time someone needs to act upon your message in order to use a product or service. This is about giving the reader a sense of urgency while understanding some of the products that will be featured in the future. Scheduling your content based on what will happen in the future is important. Give people a reason to buy something now by explaining that it will be critical down the road.

Partner with the Company You're Promoting:

Once you have a fair amount of readers (or even if you don't), many companies will be happy to offer special promotions through your affiliate marketing page. For example, many affiliate marketers offer their readers special discounts that they can only get by using their promo code or by following the special link they provide.

For example, if you're writing about the best VPN softwares out there, you may be able to negotiate a nice discount with these companies in return for promoting their service and providing an honest article about the pros and cons of using them vs. other providers. They may give you a special promo code that is customized only for your audience that gives your readers 25% off, or the first month free or something. This type of situation is a win-win for you and the company because for them, it encourages more sales, and for you, it ensures you'll get credit for the referral. If people can only get the discount by using a code or link you give them, that means the company will know exactly where their sale came from and you'll get your affiliate commission.

What Reasons Do Your Customers Have for Buying Products?

As people support your business, they will be doing so according to their wants and needs. You must tailor your content and your approach based on what visitors might be thinking. What if you were promoting a website that sells shoes? Maybe your customers are going online to look for specific types of shoes. You should prepare content that relates to the things people might consider as they aim to buy shoes from you.

Some customers might be trying to get comfortable shoes for the workplace. You could write content relating to how to find fashionable yet comfortable shoes for many working environments. Perhaps customers might want to find running shoes for their regular jogging activities. Your site might include details on how to find a good running shoe based on how the feet hit the ground while moving.

Whatever the case is, you should look at what your customers might be thinking as they buy products. They will have their own reasons for wanting to buy products through your links. Feel free to ask those customers questions. Any question will do if you just think about it. Just try to figure out what makes your visitors tick and you will be rewarded with new ideas for content.

Think about what you consider as you buy something. Are you thinking about what a product might do for you? What triggers you into even thinking of a purchase in the first place? These could be ideas you could use for your promotional articles.

Be Consistent with the Message

You must also keep your messages under control. You cannot bounce from one message to another. The greatest problem with jumping around is that it might make it harder for people to think that you understand what you want to do. People prefer it when they are reading sites that stick with a particular attitude or message. They might not be interested in a place that keeps changing its values as they might think there is a strong sense of uncertainty in how their site is being planned out.

A blog about home renovation tasks should contain details on how to make one's home look great. Talking about buying a new home or how to search for a new home would obviously be a poor idea as that does not fit in with the message of your site. Keeping a consistent approach is vital to your success. This gives the readers a reason to keep on looking at your site.

Plan your affiliate marketing work carefully. Be clear with what you are choosing and see that you have a smart layout so that it becomes easier for your site to work well. It is not hard to produce a great site when you have a clear layout and idea for how you are going to produce something worthwhile and effective for your marketing program.

Affiliate Marketing with Amazon:

1.   Step 1

Go to ClickBank.com or Amazon.com and signup for a free account. These are the most popular affiliate websites where you will get paid if someone buys a product using your affiliate link. The commission depends on a variety of factors, but ClickBank.com generally pays a lot more than what Amazon does, but again, Amazon has a lot more products to choose from, and is a lot more reputed site.

2.   Step 2

The next step is to select a good product to promote. If you select ClickBank go to your account and sort the items in order of their gravity, or payout commission amount, the one you prefer. If on Amazon, you will have to select the bestsellers, or the hottest items of the moment, and make an appropriate selection.

3. Step 3

Next step is to build a website or a blog around the product, the site that you are going to use to promote it to people and earn commissions. You can sign up for a cheap website from GoDaddy, or if you do not wish to spend any money, you can build a blog with blogger.com or WordPress.com. Then you should write some content for the site/blog using the descriptions or reviews that you find elsewhere, most commonly in the product description page of ClickBank or Amazon itself. Make it sound like you are a neutral buyer, and just suggesting others to try it. The sad reality is no one lover internet marketers!

4. Step 4

In this step, all you want to do is get your site indexed with Google. The most primary thing that you can do is to go to the various bookmarking site, and bookmark your pages. Also, do not forget to ping your site with a site called pingomatic.com. In this way, you will succeed in getting the attention of Google, and get indexed so that others find your site when they are looking for the product.

5. Step 5

Go and promote your site everywhere! Post a video on YouTube, make blog posts with other Web 2.0 properties, and indulge in discussions in other related forums. Do whatever it takes to bring traffic to your site, because it is the traffic that will determine the amount of money that you will earn from the internet.

Things You Need to Get Started in Selling Items in The Amazon Selling Platform

Amazon.com was one of the first affiliate programs which allowed you to sell books online. They are still one of the largest online retailers in the world and have an excellent affiliate program.

Today you can also make money as an affiliate doing things such as getting leads or getting people to click on ads. Google Adsense is an example of this.

Now let's look at the 3 simple affiliate marketing steps.

1. Choose a niche. Find something that you have an interest in or are passionate about.

This is good advice because you will stick with it even when you're not making money at first. It might also be something that you have knowledge on and could turn into an Internet business.

One of the tricks to making money with affiliate marketing is to brand yourself as an expert in the niche you choose. Being passionate about it, or knowledgeable on it, will help you do that.

2. Find affiliate programs. Most affiliate programs are free to join.

Merchants are looking for people to represent their products online. Finding products or programs is not hard to do. Joining and affiliate network is a good way to get started.

Google Adsense is the top pay per click affiliate program. Commission Junction is the top cost per action affiliate program..

ClickBank is the largest digital information affiliate program. Amazon is a great program to find physical products to sell.

If you join these 4 you will have plenty products to promote online. You might want to start with Google Adsense and then branch out from there.

3. Promote like crazy. You can promote the affiliate marketing website when you first get started.

Some people will start a free blog at Blogger.com which is owned by Google. This is also a fast way to get approved for the Google Adsense affiliate program.

Eventually you may want to become more

professional and host your own blog. There are many quality hosting companies such as Blue Host and Host Gator you can join.

This will involve purchasing your own domain names. Godaddy and Name Cheap are 2 good places to do that.

Use the Fantastico program that your hosting company will provide. This is a fast way to set up a WordPress blog which is the number one blogging platform in the world today.

One of the things that is good about simple affiliate marketing is it doesn't take any technical knowledge to get started. This is true whether you host your own blog or just promote your affiliate website directly.

Section 3: Dropshipping

What Is Dropshipping?

Dropshipping is when the supplier ships products straight to the customer instead of the retailer. It has been used widely by larger UK retailers for many years, a more familiar term being 'direct fulfillment'. Many catalog companies use this, for example. It's now becoming more and more available to the smaller trader.

Drop shipping has many advantages. The main advantage is that the retailer no longer needs to purchase in bulk, so there is an immediate cost advantage. Retailers avoid the risk of shelling out large sums of money on a stock that may not sell. Another major advantage is there is no need to have a large storage space for stock. Typically, the retailer sells an item on an e-commerce website, or through a magazine/leaflet order form and collects the money from the customer up front. The retailer then passes the order to the drop shipper for processing.

Drop shippers exist in many forms. They can be a manufacturer or a wholesale distributor. They can be difficult to locate, as they don't openly advertise the fact that they drop ship.

If you're looking for drop shippers on the internet, you'll be confronted by dozens of services that promise easy money using drop shipping and these services should, in the main, be avoided.

A true drop shipper is a manufacturer or authorized wholesale distributor. Anything else is a middleman. While it is possible to successfully trade with middlemen, particularly for the startup trader, it is best to try to locate the real deal to avoid being ripped off and to maximize profit. In the last few years, a number of paid services have emerged that have done a lot of the research and have built up wholesale and drop shipping databases. While the intention of these services is to provide genuine sources, it is advisable to always check out the sources they contain before commencing trading with them.

Identifying the Dropship Service That Suits You

Drop shipping is an excellent option to start an online retail venture with little investment. The products you choose to drop ship are critical to the profitability of your business. So, before you plan to create your online drop shipping store, decide on the products you are planning to drop ship. The next step would involve identifying the reliable suppliers who can drop ship the product to your consumers.

Choosing a supplier for your product is a trial and error process. The best option I would suggest would be to buy a sample product from them and analyze the quality of the product. If you are satisfied with their product, then stick to the supplier if the profit margin you could achieve is satisfactory. This is a basic step to identify a quality supplier for your product. If you are focusing on a huge number of products, identifying a reliable supplier for each of those products can become a tedious and time-consuming process.

Here is when Dropship Services come into play. The role of a dropshipping service company (or order fulfillment company) is to do all the dealings with the supplier hence reducing your effort in identifying quality suppliers. Most of the dropship services validate the authenticity of the supplier making sure you get the products on time if ordered. There are quite a few Dropship Services available namely Doba, Worldwide brands, Dropship Access, SaleHoo etc.

Before deciding on the Dropship option that is suitable for you, you need to decide the following:

- Product(s) you are planning to dropship
- Amount you could invest
- Do you prefer to try the service before subscribing?
- Are you planning to sell the products on eBay?

Most of the dropship services charge you a monthly fee or upfront one-off payment in order to use their services. If you are new to drop shipping, you can try drop ship service like Doba which offers a free 7-day trial. This would be a sufficient time to figure out whether drop ship service is suitable for you.

Your decision should be based on the availability of the product you are planning to drop ship and the suppliers you have access to. Another advantage in Doba is that it is "eBay certified" meaning you can drop ship products available through Doba on eBay.

You'll also really want to have a reliably supplier in place. Nothing will kill your online store faster than having poor quality products or miscommunications between the store and supplier. Two good options for finding suppliers is Alibaba and Aliexpress. Alibaba is a traditional network of suppliers (mainly overseas supplier and manufactures like in China), and Aliexpress is the same but offers specific products that can be ordered in quantities of "one." This means, if you set up your dropshipping store, and then use AliExpress, you can simply order the product yourself from AliExpress when someone buys the product from your store.

Pros and Cons Of Drop Shipping?

Drop shipping is a technique where the retailer does not keep goods in stock. When a customer orders goods the retailer forwards the order to the manufacturer or wholesaler and then the goods are shipped directly to the customer. Retailers make their profit by the difference in price between them and the wholesaler. There are many things to consider when looking at drop shipping for your small business.

A positive point is that you don't have to carry a lot of inventory, which means you won't need to find a place to store it. Also, don't have to invest a lot of money in the beginning on inventory as it will be ordered on a per-need basis. This will allow you to list multiple products in the beginning and then when you see which sells best you can focus on those products. Companies like Saleroom, a wholesale directory company, are now used by over 50,000 retailers, so drop shipping is becoming very popular.

However, you should be aware of potential drawbacks with dropshipping: This method of fulfilling orders is going to mean you will have some stiff competition. This could mean a lower profit margin for you unless you are able to keep your prices competitive. It is also possible for suppliers to run out of inventory which could result in disappointing your customers and possibly losing future sales. If you have relied on drop shipping for an auction site and then all of a sudden can't deliver the goods because your supplier has run out the item, it can cost you quite a bit of money and grief. Also, you need to consider the fact that if you are selling inventory online one item at a time you will get the wholesale price but if you are buying in bulk you will be able to purchase the goods at a much cheaper rate. There is also the drop shipping fee to consider and you need to be aware of that when selling your products. One of the main disadvantages to drop shipping is that you are not in control of your inventory and therefore, have to rely on other people and companies to fill your orders. It is possible that you and your customers may have issues or be disappointed. Part of the problem that sometimes arises is that the manufacturer isn't usually a customer-facing organization. They're not used to dealing directly with consumers and it's not something they normally do, so they may not be consistent or professional enough for your liking. This is why it may take some trial and error before you find that perfect manufacturer. Drop shipping can prove to be a great, inexpensive way to control inventory and start selling online. It does, however, have its downsides and these need to be considered.

The Drop Shipping Order Fulfillment Process

When you do not have enough expertise or knowledge in this regard, you should ideally recruit a consultant for advice. When you are selling custom products like items carrying a logo, your products will need some extra finishing before they can be shipped. But ordinary items do not need such extra care and can be conveniently shipped. A competent and professional fulfillment center can give a status report regarding any order to anyone wanting that information. Even if you own a warehouse you could still consider outsourcing order fulfillment. The warehouse can get congested, and there may be the need for a bigger space to keep the additional inventory or extra activity during the peak season. Also, there may be the demand for storing some types of inventories elsewhere nearer to remote buyers. Outsourcing may be the best option for you when your business is growing rapidly and you have to handle large sales volumes. As a means of cutting down on overhead expenses and costs, this is an intelligent alternative.

Expanding your market abroad becomes less risky and more lucrative. You can store the items closer to buyers and cut down on shipping expenses while at the same time making a "free shipping offer" to lure buyers. The fulfillment system can be great for small businesses, but at the same time, it needs to be nimble and flexible. For instance, you should be able to stop a sale in case that product is unavailable, or else customer satisfaction may suffer. For those dealing with huge volumes of non-perishables or only those with a small order capacity, fulfillment centers may be the right choice. Bringing the order to the buyer is as important as making the sale happen.

Of course, customer service needs to be considered as well. This can very easily be outsourced. If you want to have a dedicated email address and phone number, there are many companies that provide outsourced customer service solutions. You can be as involved or as un-involved as you want here. If you want someone to be available to field calls and emails from current, past or potential customers regarding questions about products, shipping issues, returns, refunds etc, you can easily outsource this. It may require a fair amount of work to train the people who will be handling this, but once you've put together all the relevant information for them, you won't have to do much.

You can start by creating an FAQ section on your website. You can also try to be as descriptive as possible with every product listing to reduce the number of questions. You should also clearly list your return and refund policy so people know it before they purchase the item. You should also have a system in place for making the customer aware of when their order will be shipped to them.

The Do's and Don'ts of the Fulfillment Process:

The time comes when shipping and packaging orders turns out to be a big challenge for growing e-commerce companies. During such times, outsourcing order fulfillment may be your best option. This enables smaller retailers to concentrate on marketing and product development instead of having to worry about shipping them. When you outsource your order fulfillment, you are actually being given the chance to compete with the big names in the business.

You can store a much larger volume of inventory in such warehouses and with a web-based application; it is even possible to log in to view the status of your current inventory and every item's history. Of course, with your drop-shipping store, you probably won't start out holding inventory, but if certain items start selling well, you may start purchasing and holding inventory to reduce your costs and maximize your margins.

Fulfillment houses are typically called warehouses or distribution centers that basically store inventory and ship parcels efficiently once they receive orders to do so. Shipping requests are accepted through web-based applications, whereby the invoices are mailed to the warehouse. As a customer, you can log in to view the status of any order and find your tracking number. The greatest advantage of such fulfillment centers is that you can create a vast warehouse distribution network making it possible for you to store your inventory in distant locations, take different orders from anywhere, and then ship the ordered products to buyers from the warehouse that is closest. This will automatically ensure speedier deliveries at far lesser costs and hassles.

Steps Selection Process For Drop Shippers

Drop shipping has rapidly become one of the easiest ways to sell products on the internet without the need for capital, there are many thousands of dropshipping websites and e-stores out there, just as there are many many services and tools that claim to be indispensable for the novice dropshipper. Thus, it can be a minefield for those looking to get into drop shipping in order to make some money. Here are some things to consider before getting started:

Some questions you may wish to ask are:

1.   Is the drop shipping product list static?

What I mean by this is 'are the products that are currently available going to change?' This question is important because if a drop shipper sticks to a fixed product list then you have no way of moving with the times and you will be plugging away trying to drop ship out of 'life cycle' products. Ideally, the product list should update regularly giving you different products to promote and make money from. This will be a trial and error process as well as you slowly perfect your online product offerings. Many products you try, won't sell well, but others will sell amazingly well. By doing your research and through trial and error, you will be able to build up a store of products that all sell "amazingly well." So for this reason, we don't recommend using a static product list.

2.   In regards to your manufacturers, what availability guarantees are they claiming and are they proven?

One of the key factors to consider when using a manufacturer for drop shipping is the availability of product. Remember you are selling to a customer without having the product at hand so you need to be assured that when you sell that Playstation3 or iPod that the drop shipper will have the product in stock and be able to deliver to your customer. There is nothing worse than selling a product to a customer who thinks you have the product in stock only to find out the drop shipper is out of stock and you have to let them down. I term this "Business Critical," as there is no hope of keeping that customer after letting people down. Some of the more advanced drop shippers have online access to their stock lists and you can see what they have in stock and how quickly they go out of stock before you choose to sell a particular product. They may also be working with multiple manufacturers, so they may have a back up plan if their usual supplier for a particular product is out of stock.

3.   Previous customer testimonials?

Nothing is better than word of mouth; if a previous customer is willing to praise a manufacturer, then they are obviously doing something right. That's why you may like to use websites like Alibaba and Aliexpress. By going through this network, you're getting certain protections backed by the network. You also get to see ratings for manufacturers and information about previous customer experiences with these manufacturers.

4.   Sales/Copy and images for auctions?

Does the drop shipper provide any sales copy and/or images that you can use on your sales pages? Most of the reputable ones are willing to help you in this area because the more you sell the more they sell. Some manufacturers even provide website templates and complete sites for you to install which can help if you have a limited technical ability. You MUST verify that any images or collateral you use for your business are trademark and copyright free.

Unfortunately, manufacturers aren't always reliable in this area, so you need to do your own due diligence and make sure that any images and text you're using are not copyrighted.

5. Does the pricing allow you a good margin?

When selecting a drop shipper always compare the prices they charge to those that are being commanded in your marketplace, research some offers from your competition and see whether you are comparable or hopefully better. Obviously, this is one single product and don't be afraid to use a manufacturer for one product and use another for another product, drop shipping is that easy you can use 10 different manufacturers to sell 10 different products. Note that in the beginning, your margins may not be very high yet. This is okay because you'll be experimenting with different manufacturers and different products. Once you find your key products and best manufacturers, you'll be able to make better margins, and perhaps even down the road, start purchasing inventory so that you can reduce your costs and maximize your margins.

6. How long does it take before you ship my order?

What are the lead times for the shipping of your orders, obviously your customers are expecting a speedy service and if the drop shipper in question is going to take 2-3 weeks to ship then you are not going to have many happy customers? You will also need this information so that in your sales copy you can inform the customer the expected delivery times. Most reputable drop shippers ship in 3 days maximum, with some delivering next day.

7.   Can I place orders 24/7?

This can be important especially if you are using a manufacturer in a different country, the customer in your country may purchase the product during the day, but in the country where your manufacturer is, it may be the middle of the night. As such these logistics may cause added delays if you do not have a system in place. Top line drop shippers have automated systems but other reputable drop shippers still use manual ordering so this is not a factor to put you off but more a bonus if the system is automated.

8.   How will my merchandise be shipped?

The simple question here, "is will the item be shipped in plain packaging?" Or better yet, can the item be shipped from the manufacturer or through the fulfillment company with your dropshipping logo on the box and/or invoice? Keep in mind that if the item is shipped with the manufacturers information all over the box and invoice, then the customer can circumvent you on any subsequent orders, which can easily kill off your business. Again, pretty much all the reputable drop shippers post under plain packaging but there are a few that don't and obviously, these are the ones to avoid. It is also wise to review how the drop shipper delivers, i.e. with postal service/3 rd party service they are using and the guarantees/information that they provide such as tracking codes etc. Always go with a drop shipping service that doesn't advertise themself when they ship to your customer.

9.   Do you ship internationally?

Obviously, you want to sell to the biggest market you can and if your drop shipper will not ship

Internationally then you will potentially be losing a large chunk of sales. Again this needs to be taken into context with the product you are selling, if it is a country specific product that you are just selling then international shipping is not a factor also if it is a bulky product then the shipping costs would deter most customers or if you're bearing the shipping costs, you probably wouldn't make any margin.

10.   Are they a middleman or an actual manufacturer/dropshipper?

When researching a drop shipper you want to make sure that they are actually a true manufacturer/drop shipper and not actually a middleman that is using a drop shipper to drop ship for you. This means that you are being overcharged and that with a bit more research you will be able to locate the original drop shipper and make some extra profit per sale. This can be a bit tricky—especially when you're first starting out. Manufacturers are notoriously bad at marketing themselves and often their websites look archaic and sketchy. Alternatively, savvy middlemen may have sleek websites and advertise themselves all over the internet, but they're not true dropshippers or manufacturers so even though they look more legit, they're not the ones you want to work with. They will just cut into your margin and make it difficult for you to make any money. This is why you will probably find it useful to initially use a network or service like Alibaba or Aliexpress since it offers fairly reputable information about manufacturers/dropshippers including customer ratings and company guarantees.

11.   What is the return and refund policy?

What exactly is your manufacturer's refund/return policy? If they don't accept returns, don't use them. Period. Obviously when selling any product your customer may have a problem with it or they may later feel it is actually unsuitable after all and wish to return it, this is obviously a service you may or may not actually offer to your customer, however, if your manufacturer strictly prohibits return, then you are faced with the choice of either following suit and also not allowing returns through your online store, or else you'll be forced to eat the cost if the customer returns a product. Both of these can put you at great risk, so we recommend that you only consider working with manufacturers who have a good return policyWhat generally happens is you contact the drop shipper and they issue you with a returns authority number (RA) which you need to use to send the products back, when the product arrives back then they issue a refund which you pass onto the customer.

Obviously, this adds time to the return process and in the meantime, you may wish to refund the customer as soon as they return the product to you before you send it back to your drop shipper because this will speed the customer refund and increase your customer satisfaction.

12. Do you have to reside in the same country to use the manufacturer?

Some drop shippers only allow residents of their own country to use their service and this question needs to be asked so that there is no confusion or problems going forward.

Although not a complete list these are the twelve questions that I refer back to when selecting a new drop shipping partner and they have kept me out of trouble so far. You may wish to add to this list yourself but with a few simple questions and a little bit of research you can turn your drop shipping dreams into reality and start earning some money. Drop shipping is here to stay and there are many people that say it doesn't work, but typically, these are the people that just jumped headlong into it without a product or brand strategy—or else they didn't take the time to carefully vet their partners and ended up getting burned. Many people are successfully using a number of drop shippers to serve their increasing international customer base both in a timely and customer-focused manner.

Benefits of Using A Fulfillment Network

1. Shipping has always been outsourced through courier services, but today it is easy for the customer to log onto an outsourced distribution center to check out inventory statuses.

2. Outsourcing helps retailers to focus on marketing and sales activities and overall growth plans for the company without having to think about deliveries and shipping hassles. Use this free time to expand your product lines and websites and venture into new avenues.

3. Maintaining a warehouse can be expensive because of security considerations, software developments needed to carry on the online transactions and labor issues during peak seasons. But outsourcing helps cut down on employee overhead and capital costs.

4. Shipping costs also are lowered because with a vast distribution network, now you can store your products closer to your buyer. Although this means that you have to freight more inventories, the end costs are low because bulk shipping turns out to be less expensive than parcel shipping costs. However, you won't deal with this much at the beginning since you won't be holding inventory

5. Outsourcing allows you to reach out to foreign markets by giving your buyers local shipping rate advantages, local delivery times and returns. When the buyer cannot examine a product before he pays for it, there are bound to be cases of returns or exchanges. These cases are then handled by the fulfillment centers, which review the items

and either dispose of them if they are damaged or return them back to the inventory if exchanges are needed.

6. Outsourcing helps a business to grow without having to spend colossal funds on infrastructure or employees.

Find A Dropshipping Niche

The first thing to decide is what it is you will be selling. Here, a lot of people or making a big mistake. They pick out products they themselves like. They base their decisions on personal preference and emotion instead of cold hard facts and sales stats. While that is very understandable when you have a brick and mortar business in which you have to 'live' 10 hours a day, this is not a wise move on the internet. In the wholesale drop shipping business, you do not have an inventory yourself, you do not handle the goods yourself, and so it is not important what you sell as long as you sell. In other words, it is the market that decides what you are going to sell. You have to find a so-called niche where the competition is not murderous in order to establish yourself as an online seller. If that niche happens to overlap with your personal interest, fine. But there is no point in being seller #4587 who offers children's DVD's online. Chances are you never sell a single DVD... That is a waste of time, effort and money. So you go browse and browse and browse some more on the internet to find out what it is people are looking for—something that is not available on every streetcorner. Checking google trends and other similar website will help get you started in the right direction. That might be your niche! Then you have to find out what other products in that same niche are interesting. Because in most cases you'll want to sell more than one product. But depending on how "niche" your product is, you may only want to sell related products. Some people create "general stores" online where people can buy any number of random things.

While this works for some people, we recommend having a more concrete strategy and focusing on really penetrating a specific niche. Once you decide on your niche, only consider listing products that someone in that niche would be interested in. You can easily start a different brand under a different website and list other un-related products. It's better to do that than to dilute your brand by cramming your store with unrelated products. For example, it is not a good idea to sell pet food and watches, just to name a silly combination.

You get the picture. If you are going to sell pet food then you can look for other items in the pet corner and see if there is a demand for that. Once you decided what niche you want to work with you have to find a reliable wholesale drop shipping company that does as it promises. is complaints from your customers that the goods are not delivered, not in good order or totally wrong and other similar grievances are huge red flags. If you see comments like these about a manufacturer you're considering, reconsider. So again you are going to do some research, find out what other sellers think of different companies and then you decide which one you want to do business with.

Choosing A Niche Product To Dropship

Check suppliers. Once you have some potential niche product ideas, determine your final choice by the supplier. Let's say I've narrowed down my selection to three options: studded motorcycle boots, cooking utensils, or calligraphy sets. I've checked to make sure there is a sufficient market for all three products. The best way to make my final decision is to see which niche product has the best suppliers. I can submit a research request to wholesale match, get back a list of suppliers for all three products, and then choose my favorite supplier(s) of the bunch. Maybe I'll find out that the licensed sports products suppliers have a paucity of Cubs products. Maybe I won't like the attitude of the motorcycle boots suppliers. And maybe I'll find a manufacturer with a smoking' deal on calligraphy sets: that's how I know I should go with the third option.

Create your own supplier. If you've brainstormed a truly unique niche product—one that nobody else is selling—you may encounter difficulties finding a supplier. In this case, you might have to get creative.

Let's say I choose Hebrew T-shirts as my niche product, but I can't find a single supplier with this type of shirt. What can I do? Well, all I really need is a t-shirt printer. If I can find a supplier who prints and drop ships t-shirts, I can get them printed with anything I like. The benefit of this tack is I will be the only one selling those exact t-shirts. I'll be the exclusive supplier of my product line, and there's really no better market position.

Finding a product niche is no longer difficult when you realize that almost every person on the planet has interests that can be divided into a dozen or more quirky niches. Examining your own purchase history is a great way to brainstorm product ideas because all the products you consider are ones that you know people buy online - after all, that's how you got them! You can be your own market research.

Selecting The Best Dropship Products

The kind of products you list for sale on your store will largely determine your online success as regards e-commerce. This aspect is especially quite challenging to most beginners who want to sell items on their website. Here are 4 tips on how you can select the best drop ship products for your business.

1. Low-Priced Items

As a beginner, it's not advisable that you start your dropship business by listing expensive items such as diamond jewelry and plasma screen televisions. It might be risky to think that such products will give you greater profits than low-cost products. Considering real-life situations in which most prospective buyers are usually reluctant to provide their credit card details when they are shopping for small items, do you think they will readily buy those costly items from a beginner? It's good to be conservative in product selection until you have a positive rating for your business, be it on your site or an e-commerce site like eBay. As a rule of thumb, let the highest product price be $100. In addition, don't think that it is only expensive products that can offer the highest profit margin.

2. Shipping

You also have to consider shipping costs for your products. Shipping typically inflates prices. It won't be reasonable if consumers can buy the same product in a local store for the price you offer it on your web store. Generally, ensure that you have small shipping costs for your items. Nevertheless, if you have a good supplier, you won't have to bother about shipping since many wholesale suppliers offer free shipping.

3. Niche

If you're just starting out, select a particular niche. Don't set up a general store because you may not be able to withstand competitions on wide varieties of products. Focusing on a specific niche market, you can easily promote your business through blogging and article marketing. With effective search engine optimization, you can drive massive traffic to your site. Moreover, you can easily build loyal followers for your site and blog.

4. Uniqueness

Don't try to imitate established online businesses since you won't be able to favorably compete with them. Consumers will prefer to buy from your competitor if they find out that you are doing an online business that is an exact copy of a larger business. Look for specific needs that have not been fully met in your niche. You can participate in forums and social networking sites to get some ideas.

Once you have concluded your research on the best drop ship products, you just need to find a good and reliable supplier that can deliver ordered items to your customers on time.

The first step to picking your products involves identifying your niche. It has been proven again and again that eBay sellers who focus on a niche market are much more successful both in sales from new traffic and sales from repeat customers.

Important Notes on Selection Criteria For Products

It is very easy to get overwhelmed by the many products you now have access to. Here are some crucial factors to keep in mind when choosing your niche market and the best products within your niche:

- Don't choose a niche that is already highly saturated on eBay. You can easily determine the saturation level by doing a couple of eBay searches for products in the niche you are considering. For example, if I go to eBay and search for "Cell Phones" tens and even hundreds of thousands of listings are going to pop up. Your listing would get lost in the shuffle. Search for "Underwater Camera" and you will find it is a much less crowded category. It is always a good idea to check the completed listings for a more accurate idea of how well the item is selling overall on eBay and for how much.

- When choosing products, avoid items that have a low quantity available. It may seem like an easy sell but when quantities are low you take a huge risk that the item will sell out before you sell it. In some cases, products with a low quantity are actually already sold out and have not been updated yet. You can always contact customer service to get more information as to the availability. My general rule is not to sell products that have a quantity of less than 25 in stock.

- Do eBay searches for any item you are interested in. You can see how much competition there is and also by checking the completed auctions you can get a picture of how much people are paying for the item.

Note: When doing your research, you'll see that prices can vary greatly. You may ask yourself why that is, and the answer is that it is all about the presentation and positioning. It's how you brand yourself: do you want to be seen as the high-end brand? The Budget Brand? Mid-range? Or something else? Generally, people will want to feel like they're getting more value if they're paying more, so that's something you have to consider in your pricing strategy. Often it's a mistake with new drop-shippers to under-price their items. You need a differentiating factor other than price that will motivate buyers. Don't try to compete on price, because you will usually lose to the bigger guys who can purchase and distribute the same goods cheaper than you can because of their manufacturer relationships and MOQ (Minimum Order Quantity) tier pricing.

Setting Up Your Dropshipping Business

Drop shipping is like any business and the most important thing when starting out on any venture is to do your market research FIRST...When you open a store in your town; you wouldn't open it without doing your market research first. The same thing applies if you are going to sell something on the internet as a drop shipper. Not only are there billions of web pages out there that could be selling competitive products, the net changes so fast that you are obsolete as soon as you have gotten started. If you are going to set up a drop shipping business you want to make sure that the product that you choose can be easily sold. And you want to know how many competitors you have. And you want to stay as up to date as possible. Selling products on the Internet is easy. Hundreds of thousands of people do it every day online on auction sites such as eBay.

The most difficult part of internet sales is getting the products delivered to the customer, otherwise known as order fulfillment. You must have an efficient fulfillment system. One of the reasons that brick-and-mortar stores are so slow on the uptake when it comes to online business is that supplying retail stores is done with pallet-sized orders usually. But internet sales require an entirely different kind of fulfillment system. Selling on the internet is essentially mail order, with shipments going out in small parcels to end users.

I know that you are excited to open up your online store and I congratulate you for all the effort that you put into conducting product and market research, and designing your website. That's why I want to share these important points before you launch your online business. It might not directly contribute to your sales, but will definitely influence your buyers to trust you.

1.   Business entity
You have to officially register your online business with a name which will be recognized by the government.

For some countries, you don't have to register, but in the United States, there are two ways on how you can register your online business. You could either register it as a corporation or fictitious name. Normally if you register as a corporation you have to pay $90.00 for processing which you can submit online. While registering under a fictitious name, the average cost of registration is $35.00. The latter will not provide the same protection with a former form of registration. The second is also known as DBA or "Doing Business As" and usually obtained from the local country office. If you are not certain what to choose, try consulting your attorney or accountant.

2.   Business license

Aside from filing your business entity you also need to file a license to operate your online business to your local government. There are some county governments who will require you to do so like Florida, but still, there are some countries and counties that will not. They would either call it "Business License" or "County Occupational".

3.   Business bank account

Like any other businesses whether online or offline, you must open a bank account for your business. It is ideal to open a separate business account for your online drop shipping business from your personal account.

4.   Merchant account

As an online businessman who uses drop shipping,

you need to open a merchant account for your business. Since the majority of the payments are done through credit cards your merchant account will allow you to accept credit cards from your customers online. This is the most efficient way to get paid by your customers rather than a money order or money transfer. Even customers prefer using credit cards because of surcharges involve in using other modes of payments. You don't have to worry setting up your merchant account into your online store because your merchant banker will provide you the assistance needed to set it up.

How to Start Dropshipping Successfully:

When the orders are received, the reseller supplies the information regarding the buyers' names and addresses and other details of the order, so that the supplier can send the products to the buyer. The company also collects the payment. The business of drop ship services can reap rich returns for the business owner, but the most important dropshipping guide is that it is necessary to take care of the business and customers to ensure that any buyers' complaints regarding poor product quality or delays between receipt of payments and delivery of goods are tended to promptly. Any negligence in providing necessary after-sales services and attending to complaints can tarnish the image of the company and lead to loss of revenue and future orders. In order to find an answer to how to drop ship and how to start a drop shipping business, it is vital to select a reliable supplier. The wrong selection can have disastrous results. Follow the following tips before starting this type of business.

Factors to Consider in Choosing Your Manufacturing Partner:

1.   Select recommended suppliers: The first tip for starting a drop ship services business is that the sourcing of the suppliers should be done with great care. Simply select the suppliers recommended by other people. It is possible to get free or paid-for lists of drop shipping companies on Internet directory sites. Some give accurate information whereas others might be owned by unscrupulous suppliers, so avoid those particular recommendations.

2.   Check the contact details: Once a selection is made based on reliable recommendations, and after checking that the range of products that the business intends to deal are sold by the supplier, check the contact details provided by the supplier. Pertinent contact information such as phone number, email address, and a mailing address should be available on the supplier's website. Avoid any supplier with incorrect or with no contact information at all. Make sure the phone is answered and see how long it takes for the supplier to answer emails, which may come in handy later if you have a reason to contact them with a problem.

3.   Check business terms: Since there can be disputes with the supplier regarding faulty goods or undelivered items, business terms and conditions of the supplier should be properly stated and understood by the reseller. Realize that the responsibilities of the business as a reseller are different than the responsibilities that the supplier would have toward the reseller.

4.   Unreasonable subscription fees: As a reseller, the dropship services business has to pay resellers registration fees and, in some cases, ongoing subscription charges for the right to access the supplier's catalog. Access for a limited time is normally allowed before registration. Before registering with any supplier, check whether it charges ongoing subscription fees. Fine print should also be checked well for any between-the-lines clauses.

5.   Beware of middlemen disguised as suppliers: Check whether the potential supplier holds enough stock of the products and they are not a middleman posing as a supplier. These middlemen place orders with the real supplier and when they receive orders from the reseller and, in this process, long delays can take place. These delays can result in losses to the customer and subsequent losses to the reseller because the payment would have to be refunded.

6.   Modes of payment: Find out how the supplier expects to receive payments because the most convenient mode would be the same by which the customer pays the

reseller. This will save charges and time. It is also advisable to avoid having to pay by Wire Transfer or Telegraph Transfer because the risk is higher if there is no customer protection.

7.　　Beware of companies selling fake goods: While choosing a supplier, avoid those sites that offer branded goods such as designer clothing and electrical goods at unbelievably low prices. Such low priced, so-called designer goods are bound to be fake unless the supplier is trustworthy and renowned and he has obtained the goods from a close-out, or if the goods are refurbished or Grade A returns. If the reseller sells fake goods, he can be accused of selling counterfeit goods.

8.　　Look for web reviews: Having short-listed a few suppliers, it would be helpful to seek out reviews and comments regarding the companies on Internet forums from other dropship resellers. Although it might be difficult to find any good comments since the resellers would not like others to know about their profitable source, bad reviews can certainly help in making the right decision.

9.　　Look for artists and craftsmen: Teaming up with artists and craftsmen for their creative products is a unique way to do drop ship services business. These creative people usually lack marketing savvy. Visits to local craft fairs can provide unlimited opportunities to get stunning creative items at unbelievably low prices as compared to eBay prices.

The dropship business need not buy these items, but an arrangement could be worked out for working on commission. They will likely be happy to take his payment and deliver the products to the buyer of the dropship business when a sale is made.

Tips on Successfully Handling Your Dropshipping Business

When you are involved in a drop shipping business, promoting your products is essential. As the old saying goes, if Moses won't come to the mountain the mountain will come to Moses. You have to find a way to reach out to your customers and not just to wait for your luck to come in.

This means you have to learn how to reach out to your customers. Today, thanks to technology, communication, and marketing has never been easier or more accessible. You can use emails or text messages to keep up, with your customers giving them updates on discounts, or soon to be available products that you'll offer. Customers will feel valued and alternatively, you'll be actively marketing your new products/goods.

In a drop shipping business, everything is interdependent. One thing affects the other. You must monitor the flow of each item, which is the most saleable or not. Maintaining a steady communication with your supplier and at the same time monitoring your sale flow will help you add and remove products. For example, you can remove a product that is not moving and you can ask your supplier if there are other products that might be a hit to your consumers. You could also ask for an additional supply of products that are saleable. This way you won't run out of stock.

Most importantly you need to find the right people that could give you a heads up on the in's and out's of drop shipping. SaleHoo can provide you with consultations on how you can start our business. It is an online Directory that gives you tools for your foundation as a seller. It's up to you on how to choose those tools. Choose well!

Another thing to remember is to add your profit margin over the wholesaler's price. Your profit will be the difference between wholesaler's price and your customer's order price. You can benchmark your price with other suppliers to make sure that your pricing is competitive in the market. Good marketing skills are a paramount in this business; it will allow you to withstand market competition.

Reasons to Avoid Dropshipping When Selling on Ebay

Every day I get people asking me why drop shipping is not good for eBay and every day I give them the same list of five reasons:

The bottom line is that drop shipping and eBay are a toxic combination. While eBay is the place to sell products to people who want a deal, drop shipping is the way to buy products at the highest possible "wholesale" price.

And, while your drop shipper may offer thousands of products -- they probably have thousands of clients like you who are also listing the items on eBay. It simply doesn't work.

1.   Profit margin is low

The profit margin you will face when using drop shipping to sell on eBay is most often zero. Nothing. Nada. In fact, most people who first try using a drop shipper to supply their eBay products end up getting frustrated and crying "the price my drop shipper is selling the product for is MORE than the price the product is selling for on eBay." And they are correct. You see wholesale is all about buying in quantity. When you use drop shipping you are buying just one of an item and cannot expect a wholesale price. Now why paying a bit more for an item may not be a big deal if you're selling it for top dollar at your local store, it is a HUGE deal when trying to sell on eBay. eBay is a place people go to get a deal. They do not want to pay the full retail price, and chances are they can find the item at a rock bottom price if they just look around eBay for a bit. Because even if you cannot sell an item for the lowest possible price (because you are using drop shipping), there are thousands of other eBay sellers who can. So it is true. The price you get from your dropship supplier will often be more than the product sells for on ebay.

2.   Direct from the source competition

This is a relatively new phenomenon that has come about by the recent explosion of "direct from China" drop shippers. Simply put, this means that many of these drop shipping companies are actually selling the items on eBay directly themselves. They are "double dipping". While they provide a website that will drop ship products to your eBay customers direct from China, they are also selling the same products on eBay themselves. To witness this one only needs to look in the electronics category on eBay. Many of the listings have the item location show Hong Kong or some other location in China. Yes, the drop shippers themselves are competing with their customers.

3.   PayPal will hold your funds

About a year ago, in January of 2008, ebay and PayPal issued some new policies. One of which is to put a HOLD on funds. Here is thequote from eBay's policy: "In a small percentage of cases where it has been determined the risk of dissatisfied buyers is higher, PayPal may delay release of the payment funds to the seller until the buyer has left a positive feedback or 21 days have passed without a dispute, claim, chargeback or reversal filed on that transaction." Any new ebay seller who tries using drop shipping as a method for sourcing their products will find that they cannot access their funds until after the product has arrived at their customer's door.

This eliminates one of the most appealing aspects of

drop shipping - the ability to sell a product and then use the buyer's payment to fund the purchase. With PayPal holding your money for 21 days this will not be possible.

4.   Out of stock equals bad feedback

Drop shippers often run out-of-stock on popular items. This means that after you sell the item on eBay and then go to your supplier to have the item drop shipped you learn that the item is not in stock. You then have to tell your buyer the bad news and will usually get some bad feedback in return. The ebay forums are filled with sellers who have been destroyed by the bad feedback they received by trying drop shipping. They are also filled with complaints from buyers who did not receive the item they ordered because the seller was using a drop shipper -- and after the sale informed the buyer that the item was not available.

To review, drop-shipping can be one of the most rewarding and lucrative ways to make money online if you know what you're doing. It's a low-risk way to start your online store and build a brand.

To be successful, you need to have:

- A great niche product or selection of products
- A top-notch manufacturing partner that is willing to give you decent rates
- A fulfillment strategy (how will you get this product to your customers once they order it), plus an optional plan in place to start purchasing inventory

down the road if business is good and you wanted to get better rates from manufacturers

• A solid branding strategy for how you want to position your products: how will you stand out from your competition

• A well-formed active marketing strategy that will draw customers to your store. A passive strategy that simply waits for customers to find you will not work in the beginning when you have no brand loyalty or recognition.

Section 4: Selling Digital Products

Information marketing

In technical terms, Info marketing is selling information through ebooks, books, audio books, podcasts, webinars, vlogs, online courses etc.
If you go deeper, what info-marketers are really selling.
guess what?

Improvement

The number one reason anyone buys an info product is to improve some area of their life or some part of themselves. People want to learn and that's why they buy info products. People want to learn because they want to solve their problems and improve whatever it is that they want to improve.

Why today is the best time to do information marketing?

I won't give you vague reasons because that will probably confuse you. What I will show you are the statistics to prove that the information marketing and consulting industry is growing like gangbusters.

From the 2013 statistics, ebook sales are growing at a 71% rate PER YEAR. Fiction sales have dropped by 15% and if you come to think of it, 90% of the human population doesn't even read ebooks at the moment. But that is changing as the entire world is coming online and is developing a voracious appetite for e-education.

The personal coaching and self help industries are growing at a staggering 10% per year and as a $13 BILLION industry it's probably a good idea to get a piece of that cake.

Another thing that is great about this market is that it allows the small guys like us to start to build a business with a much lower barrier to entry.

Finding a highly profitable niche market

There are only 3 steps to succeed in this business.

3 Step Process

1. Evaluating what you know
2. Targeting a niche market that aligns with this area of expertise (or an area where you can become an expert) where you can solve their problems and frustrations.
3. Creating a valuable information product and selling it.

A.   Evaluating what you know

In order for you to know what your skills, talents and knowledge are that you can share with other people, let's do an exercise.

"Discovering Your Goldmine" exercise:

1. List 10 complaints that you always hear from your friends, officemates and family? Do you think you have a creative solution to any of these complaints?

2. Are these problems in the category of *HEALTH, MONEY* and *RELATIONSHIPS?* (if they are, then you have a much bigger chance of making a lot of money)

3. For each complaint write down your best technique for solving these problems.

Quick note: If you are already doubting yourself because you don't have any formal education on these topics then STOP. You don't need any formal education or badge or certificate to be a guru. Most people do not care about any of that. What they care about is "can you solve their problems?".

B.   Targeting a niche market where you can solve their problems and frustrations.

What you must understand is NICHES are not PEOPLE. Yes, they are comprised of people, but if we dive deep then we will find out that NICHES are really PROBLEMS.

Stop thinking of niches as a group of people and start thinking of it as a **GROUP OF *People With A Specific Problem That They Want To Solve Or Needs they want Met.***

If you did the goldmine exercise, then you already have a target niche.

C.   Creating a valuable information product that you can sell

People don't give a damn about your expertise. What people care about is what you can teach them to solve and meet their needs, desires, aspirations, and dreams. So, when you start creating and selling your information product stop focusing on yourself and start focusing on your customers.

Most valuable and expensive information products have steps, procedures, techniques and systems. If you outline your product under this umbrella, it'll be much more valuable from the customer's perspective. Also, a piece of advice.

Sell What They Want. Give Them What They Need.

Do you know what this means? It requires some creative marketing, but it's the key to almost any business.

Consumers are irrational and often think they want something but they actually want/need something else. If you can advertise that you will give them what they want, and then instead give them what they actually need, not only will they be more satisfied, but they just might become loyal life-long customers because you solved their problem better than they could have hoped. This is because you knew their problem better than they knew it themselves.

Here's an example: say you want to start an online travel agency. You want to start selling tours to Italy. You may advertise that you'll take people to Venice and Rome and you'll see the Colloseum and all the big highlights. This is what people think they want and this is what they're looking for online. If they see that you can make this travel dream come true for them, they'll be willing to listen to you.

Then when you take them on the trip, people may be a bit disillusioned. They might arrive at the colloseum and see how over-commercialized it is and how overcrowded it is with tourists brandishing selfie-sticks, and they'll think, "wow, this isn't like I pictured it." And they'll be a bit disappointed. They may not resent you, because you fulfilled your end of the bargain, but this will not make them life-long customers. This will not make them your champion customers that will sing your praises to all their friends and encourage everyone they know to book a trip with your company. That's what you want, right? So instead, find a way to give the customer what they really want: an unforgettable, unique trip that they simply could not have had with anyone else. Here's some ideas of a better approach: they want to see the colloseum, so instead of loading them up on a tour bus and carting them off there, perhaps you can arrange an early morning viewing or after hours where there are way fewer tourists.

Or perhaps you can briefly stop by at the colloseum, but then whisk them away to some hidden gem in Rome that most tourists don't know about where they can get their own little piece of paradise. They will have an unforgettable experience and will realize that no other company could have given them what you gave them. Not only will this make them loyal customers, but they will probably tell all their friends and you will get lots of word-of-mouth referrals.

Create Something Everyone Will Want to Buy

Being inspired is a great way to come up with ideas. Steve Jobs founder of Apple Computers is an inspiration for hundreds of businesses, Maxine Clark founder of Build a Bear Workshop is another great inspiration. These people took an idea and ran with it to give you an example. They took risks and found a niche that nobody else had filled.

Get inspired. Look around you. Do you have a product sitting there you just can't do without? How complicated is it to use? Can you teach someone else how to use it? Who made it? What is their story? These are all great questions to ask when trying to create a new product or idea. Allow inspiration to guide you to the next great idea.

Teaching people how to do something is one of the easiest ways to make money. We live in an information based world. The problem is, since Google has been around, people do not know where to even start looking for this information. Google is bogged down with so much fluff now it is your job to provide them with useful information they can use and apply.

The Biggest Mistake Ever.

I've been hammering this throughout this book because it's really important. It is in my opinion the biggest mistake even veterans make.

Most experts try to sell THEMESELVES and their EXPERTISE.

I can't say this enough, DO NOT DO THIS unless you're a celebrity or a public figure (or aspiring to become one).

If you'll apply only one thing from this book, then this must be it.

While there will be an inevitable amount of "selling yourself" when you try to connect with your market, you need to create a separation between you and your business. You are not your business. You personally may not have that much experience, but people are buying your product or service, they're not buying you.

The Biggest Niches

In this part, I will outline the biggest niches you could target and why.

First of all, there are 3 MEGA NICHES and under their umbrella are the Niches that we can target.

The 3 mega niches are HEALTHY, MONEY and RELATIONSHIPs. At the moment, they are probably the source of 99% of income of information marketers.

NOTE: I am not in any way giving you this list as advice, this is for information purposes only and I am not claiming you will make money if you pursue one of these niches. I am also not a lawyer and a doctor to give you any medical or legal advice in these topics.

Health and Fitness

Natural Weight Loss

As a society obsessed with weight loss, why not take advantage of this trend? The chemicals and pills industry isn't going to die any time soon but more and more people are looking for ways to naturally lose weight.

Stress Management

We are stressed more than ever. The society takes pride in working 12 hours a day and people are seeing it as normal. That's insane! We can create information products that can teach people how to lessen their stress and be more alive.

Muscle Gain

This is also a long-term trend that will continue to grow. In fact, some people are pretty much obsess in gaining muscle. If we narrow this down, we can even come up with the gain six pack abs niche.

Easy Exercises

I hate to say this but people are lazy. They don't want 3 hour workouts. What they want are easy exercises that can be as effective as a 3-hour exercise. If you can teach them something like that then you have a winner.

Fat Loss – Belly

The dreaded fat belly, girls hate it especially when it's their own belly we're talking about.

Organic Food

Everybody's getting sick because of food these days. People are starting to join the organic food revolution. Sooner or later people will start to demand that they're food be organic. Also, try to narrow this down and you can also come up with juicing fruits and vegetables, creating smoothie recipes etc. Narrow it down even more and you will discover more hidden gold.

Natural Healing

Times are changing and we are going back to the old way of getting healed. Western medicine is dying and in my opinion the large corporations from the medicine industries will try to kill this niche market. Don't be afraid to go in this niche, good guys always win and people will realize how scammy the western medicine industry really is.

Any Specific Health Problems

If you can help people solve a specific health problem, it can be a huge money maker. Example of these health (body) problems are candida and osteoporosis. If you can teach them best practices to solve these problems, then you are in for a treat.

Spiritual Health

Meditation, yoga, mindfulness etc.—these are all things that are wildly increasing in popularity. An ever-increasing number of people are interested in self-improvement through spiritual well-being. Are you someone that can help them improve spiritual health?

WARNING: *Again, I am not in any way giving you this list as advice, this is for information purposes only and I am not claiming you will make money if you pursue one of these niches. I am also not a lawyer and a doctor to give you and medical and legal advice in these topics.*

Relationships& Dating

1. Dating Advice

As humans, we are pre-wired to find a mate. In this modern society we call it dating or trying to find a date. We want to meet people to find a mating partner. If you can help someone improve their dating life, then you have another winner.

2. Romantic Relationships

People want their relationships to be harmonious and at the same time exciting. Teach people how to get the most of their relationship.

3. Marriage

Marriage is the ultimate relationship. It is a lifetime commitment to a person and fulfilling that commitment is pretty hard. If you can help these people build a stronger bond, it would be a great business to be with. You are helping people and you are earning money at the same time. What a noble way to make a living.

4. Sex

Humans love to have sex. Teach them make the most out of it. Many people have difficulties when it comes to sex, and it's such a personal matter that many people feel they have no one to talk to about it. The anonymity that comes with online coaching can make people more likely to seek this type of coaching/consulting online as opposed to in-person.

5. Conflict in relationships

It doesn't matter if it's conflict with family, friends, business partners, boyfriend and girlfriend, wife and husband. Teach them how they can get through these conflicts and you will be rewarded. Remember, niches are problems. Solve them.

Under the umbrella of Conflicts could also be the ultimate marriage conflict. Divorce. It is also a billion-dollar industry.

6. Parenting

Everybody wants to be a good parent. If you have passion for helping kids be better, then this is probably for you. Teach their parents and you will help their kids also.

7. Conflicts, People and Business.

Teaching the psychology of anything can help people understand why they do what they do.

8. Education in anything

It can be teaching people how to code. Teaching people how to sing, how to play the guitar. It could be anything as long as people are searching for it.

Business and Money

1. Personal Finance

People are concerned more than ever when it comes to their personal finance. You can teach them how to save, how to budget, how to build their retirement account and how to get out of debt

2. Investing

There are hundreds of niches within this niche. It could be investing in real estate, foreign exchange, investing in gold and silver, stocks, stock trading etc.

3. Starting a business

There are hundreds of different ways to make money. It could be selling on ebay, teaching them how to make money as a freelancer. In fact, this book is under this niche, information marketing is a way to start a business. Other niches are Affiliate marketing, making money through adsense. If you have a business on a certain market, then teach them how to do it. Example is teaching them how to start a restaurant, starting a a hot dog stand. Whatever, there are millions of ways to make money.

4. Marketing

Marketing today sucks. Most marketing agencies have no idea what they are doing, they just slap ads and if it looks great on tv they assume that it's great advertising. What a disgrace. Real marketing should be base on trackable results. It's called direct response marketing. If you can teach or apply this to any business, then you won't ever be hungry.

5. *Career*

People are losing their jobs. Nobody's hiring anymore. If you can find a way to help these people, then you will be a very very rich and happy man.

Find ways to build a better resume, teach them how to answer interviews. In fact, I have a book about this, it's called the "The Perfect Resume".

Special Niches

Aside from these niches, there are niches that doesn't exist in the past that are available today. The very best example I can give you is the PREPPER niche. With the rise of popularity of The Walking Dead and all those zombie movies, people are starting to prepare for it. It may sound silly to you but these people are irrationally passionate about these things. It's not just zombies by the way, it could be a certain disease or a nuclear war. It could be anything.

Narrowing

Once you got your niche, it's time to narrow it down even more.

So instead of focusing on, let's say, "organic food", why not narrow it down to "organic foods -> Organic foods preparation for our kids -> organic foods that kids love and are easy to prepare".

Now that's a more targeted niche. I'm not saying it's a good niche, I'm just giving you example of how to narrow down your target market.

Remember, when choosing a niche. SELL WHAT THEY WANT.

What people want in organic foods is for it to be:

1. Easy to prepare
2. As cheap as possible
3. They can still eat their favorite foods (organic style)

If you can give them these 3 things, then you'll have a better chance of creating a successful business.

Creating Your Product Fast

If you want to create your product as fast as possible then these are the methods I recommend. These methods assume that you don't have any knowledge or experience in your niche.

1. Licensing

Find other people that are already selling in your market. Give them a higher cut if you have to, remember you are just starting out and the more you build your network the more chances of you making a killing in this niche.

2. Ghoswriting

If you only have a little bit of knowledge on your niche, then this could be a good idea. Don't be cheap and hire the best.

You can find a variety of writer in elance.com and Upwork.com

3. Interview an expert

- Find authors on amazon
- Email them
- Ask them for an interview and ask questions that your customers want to be answered.
- Record it and BOOM!, you now have a product.
- Transcribe this and you now have an audio cd and ebook course

4. Become the Expert

Read a few books and attend a few courses and you are already more knowledgeable than 99% of your market

Start A Company That Will Grow

Now that you have a product in mind, to be successful you need to have more than just that one product. Being able to grow your company is the most important step you can take in starting a successful business.

Study any successful company. People return to them for either the same product or a different product that compliments the first one they bought. When you are done with one you will return to get more. So now your job is to come up with some related products to compliment your existing one.

I know what some of you are thinking. Is this really necessary? The answer to that is in most cases, yes. I do not think I have ever come across a successful company that only carried one product. And the great thing about Info-Products is that often, your customers will become repeat customers. But they can only become repeat customers if they have other products to buy. This will in turn possibly create backend sales so if someone buys a book from me and is happy they will hopefully return and buy more from me in the future. Same goes for my books that I have written if you like what you have read hopefully I have other titles you will also like and purchase.

These are things you need to think about in your initial stages of startup. More products will probably come in time, but without a solid backbone of at least two or three products, you will not grow into a successful business because you will have nothing to offer your return customers.

Remember, thinking of the big picture is crucial in starting a successful business. Thinking only short-term can often set you up for failure. Plan ahead for growth and you will be much closer to success than if you did not plan ahead.

Conclusion

Of the many many ways to make money online, I wanted to highlight the "Big 4" for you and really go in-depth on each of them so that you not only understand the concepts, but so that you understand what it taks to be successful in these businesses.

If you're someone that likes physical products and perhaps you even have product ideas of your own, Drop-Shipping is a great way to get started in the physical products business. It's a pretty low-risk easy way to get your feet wet. You will gain lots of experience in finding, vetting, and managing manufacturing partners, solidifying an order fulfillment process, and most of all in finding, satisfying, and retaining customers. From here, the sky's the limit. You can start buying inventory of your best-selling products and housing it in warehouses to cut supply and fulfillment costs thus maximizing your margins. Down the road, you can even start your own operations. If you want to start producing your own products, you can have that as your long-term goal and use the money you make in drop-shipping to fund that project. Who knows, someday, your brand may become a house-hold name and it will have all started with a simple one-man drop-shipping e-store.

If you're a content writer and you have a lot of information to share on a particular topic, blogging can be a fantastic way to generate interest about your writing, and make money and establish a following in the process. You can become the ultimate authority in your niche and rank in search engines simply by having quality and unique content. If you have words to share with the world, consider starting, developing and monetizing a blog. You may soon be earning enough to quit your day job.

Affiliate marketing is one of the lowest-risk ideas. There are so many ways to go about it and the more creative you are, the more likely you are to beat your competition. It could be as simple as making youtube videos where you post video-reviews of electronics with affiliate links in the description. You could start a blog about a particular topic and write informative articles and listicles with links for products, tools, and online courses/info products where people can learn more or find what they need to solve their problem. Keep in mind that as an affiliate partner for info-products, consulting, and online courses, you could stand to earn a really high commission (up to 50% of sales) if you can deliver customers. If you're good at selling people on something and you're a gifted writer that's passionate about a profitable niche topic, this is a great way to start your online empire.

Info products have quickly become the "darling" of e-commerce. All of the experts will tell you that if you can get into the info-product business, you should spare all excuses and do it now. Everyone is looking for information on the internet and if you can offer something that will solve their problem, people will be willing to listen, and many of those people will be willing to pay for your solution. This can be as simple as creating a website offering some type of consulting service. If there's anything you're an expert on, or if there's anything you really feel like people are always looking for guidance with, that could be your starting point. Creating digital products is another great way to build a business: ebooks, downloadable tools, online courses, software products etc. Best of all is if you can create a product or service that requires a subscription, you will have many life-long customers that enroll and subscribe. This can quickly become a sustainable business that you can continue to grow and build upon for years to come.

Any way you slice it, there's never been more opportunity and a better time to start an online business. No matter who you are, I feel confident that you have the ability to make one or more of these business models work for you, and remember: they're all very-low risk. You don't really need funding, or large amounts of start-up capital. You just need some good ideas, a good work ethic and perseverance. What you stand to gain far outweighs what you might have to invest. If you are longing for a life of freedom, passive income, the ability to quit your job, or supplemental income for your family, today's your day. The online world is ready for you, are you ready to enter the world of e-commerce?